IN FOCUS

W9-DDD-608

CHILE

A Guide to the People, Politics and Culture

Nick Caistor

LATIN AMERICA BUREAU

INTERLINK BOOKS
NEW YORK

© 1998   Nick Caistor   All rights reserved.
First published in 1998

In the U.S.:

Interlink Books
An imprint of Interlink Publishing Group, Inc.
99 Seventh Avenue, Brooklyn, New York 11215

Library of Congress Cataloging-in-Publication Data

Caistor, Nick
    Chile in focus: a guide to the people, politics and
    culture /by Nick Caistor
       p. cm.   (In focus)
    Includes bibliographical references and index.
    ISBN 1-56656-231-7   (pbk)
    1. Chile - Guidebooks. 2. Chile - Description and travel I. Title
    II. Series: In focus (New York, N.Y.)
    1998

                          CIP

In the U.K.:

Latin America Bureau (Research and Action) Ltd,
1 Amwell Street, London EC1R 1UL

The Latin America Bureau is an independent research and publishing
organization. It works to broaden public understanding of issues of
human rights and social and economic justice in Latin America and the
Caribbean.

A CIP catalogue record for this book is available from the British
Library
ISBN: 1 899365 18 4

Editing: James Ferguson
Cover photograph: Julio Etchart/Reportage
Cover design: Andy Dark
Design: Liz Morrell
Cartography and diagrams: Kees Prins and Marius Rieff

Already published in the *In Focus* series:
Argentina, Bolivia, Brazil, Colombia, Costa Rica, Cuba, Eastern
Caribbean, Ecuador, Jamaica, Mexico, Peru, Venezuela

Printed and bound in Korea

CONTENTS

INTRODUCTION: THE COST OF SUCCESS

Chile today is the envy of many countries in Latin America. Its economy has grown steadily in the last decade, averaging annual growth of over six per cent in the 1990s. Levels of poverty, according to the government, have halved in the last ten years. Chilean exports now reach every corner of the world: Chilean grapes decorate tables in the United States, Chilean wines are drunk from Vancouver to Newcastle; Chilean blackberries are transported halfway round the world and appear on supermarket shelves all over Europe. Chilean capital is expanding abroad, being used to buy up companies in Argentina, Peru, even Brazil. Two successive civilian presidents appear to have set the seal on a lasting return to democratic rule, in which Chileans may disagree politically, but will not take to the streets to fight for their views.

A generation ago, things were very different. The early 1970s saw President Salvador Allende and his Popular Unity government trying to find the "Chilean path to socialism." Their attempts attracted the attention of people all over the world, many of whom saw this parliamentary approach to revolution as a more viable model than the Cuban one of guerrilla warfare and one-party rule. But this hope proved an illusion, and in the end it was the U.S.-based armed intervention of a dictator and his supporters which dramatically changed the lives of an entire generation of Chileans and made the country sadly familiar to many more people in countries around the globe.

General Pinochet became the symbol of retrograde, bloodthirsty dictatorship. But when his plans to continue in power were defeated in the late 1980s, over 40 per cent of Chileans still supported him: more than had ever voted for Allende, as the general's sympathizers pointed out. It was under his rule that the economic policies which are so praised today were initiated, with their insistence on privatization, the curtailing of the welfare state, the undermining of labor, and the promotion of the individual consumer as the final arbiter. The civilian politicians who have followed the general in power have not challenged these basic assumptions, but, as one senior official has said, have seen their main goal as being "to lay the foundations of a stable, competitive, non-confrontational political system."

This approach has led to considerable economic success. But it has also thrown up many problems, which range from the increasingly damaging impact of rapid growth on Chile's environment to the fact that this ideal of competition without confrontation leaves many sectors of society on the

Mapuche indian   *Julio Etchart/Reportage*

sidelines. Those who suffer most, as ever, are the indigenous peoples like the Aymara or the Mapuche who have always had a different vision of what constitutes progress and social organization.

But even for the majority of the population, competition has led to a growth of inequality. On the one hand, the rich increasingly live in ghettos or bunkers, afraid of the violence of those excluded from the bright new world of consumerism. On the other, those who have not competed as successfully are told that shortages and poverty are a personal rather than a political problem. Money and possessions have now become the almost exclusive yardstick of individual worth, in a society which once appeared to offer other values which bound Chileans together in a unique way. In the following pages, we focus on how those other values of community and solidarity emerged from the interaction of land, history, and politics in Chile, in the hope that they can find a way of re-asserting themselves in a more truly rich, humane, and sustainable way than at present.

1   LAND AND PEOPLES: FROM DESERT TO FJORD

Noche, nieve y arena hacen la forma
de mi delgada patria,
todo el silencio está en su larga línea

Night, snow and sand make up the form
of my thin country,
all silence lies in its long line
— Pablo Neruda, *Discoverers of Chile,* 1950

Chile, one writer has observed, is so thin that everyone there has to walk sideways as in an Egyptian frieze. This may be a poetic exaggeration, but it does contain an element of truth. Chile is a country 25 times longer than it is wide. Its physical borders are very definite ones. To the west is the vast length of the Pacific Ocean; to the east, Chile is the only country in Latin America completely cut off from the rest of the continent by the Andes mountain range which runs down from Venezuela for more than 3,500 miles (both Peru and Ecuador, for example, spread beyond the mountains into the Amazon basin). This gives a sense of isolation to the country, in the minds of visitor and inhabitants alike. Then again, even today there is only one major north-to-south route, the Pan-American highway, with other roads coming off it like spurs. As another saying has it: "In Chile, you travel north to south; west and east, you go for a stroll."

Rivers are also short and cut the country east to west as they plunge down the Andean slopes out to the ocean. Much of the coastline, especially in the north, is made up of cliffs several hundred feet high, which means that ports are few and far between. Further south, this coastal range of mountains comes inland and cuts the towns of the central valley off from the shoreline. Beyond the southern port of Puerto Montt, this mountain feature becomes a chain of islands, the most important of which is Chiloé. Nowadays, the country is divided into twelve numbered administrative regions, which often use the east-west rivers as boundary points.

The Great North

Chile's climate is extraordinarily diverse and literally a question of degrees, changing from area to area as one travels south. The country's northern border, conquered from Peru and Bolivia in the War of the Pacific from 1879-1883, starts well within the Tropic of Capricorn. The rainfall

The Atacama desert in flower
after unusual rains

*Peter Francis/
South American Pictures*

here is so low that in some years none at all is registered. The hot, arid conditions have created one of the most inhospitable regions in the world: the Atacama desert. This is the *norte grande*, the great north, which occupies about a quarter of all Chile's land surface. It is also vital to its economy, as it is here that vast copper and other mineral deposits are exploited. The population is mostly to be found in ports on the Pacific coast, such as the border town of Arica or the busy nitrate and fishing port of Iquique (where earlier this century fourteen years went by without a single drop of rain).

It is also here that the mountains of the Chilean Andes are at their highest, with several peaks over 19,500 feet high. The highest peak in Chile is the Nevado Ojos del Salado at 22,609 feet, and the tallest volcano Llullaillaco, which reaches 22,104 feet. In all, there are more than 2,000 volcanoes. Almost half of them are active to some degree or other, but the main geological problem for Chile is the seismic activity which they cause, not only in the north, but throughout the country. Although this has given rise to what is supposedly the world's most boring news headline ("small earthquake in Chile: not many dead"), the reality is very different, with violent quakes causing havoc and great loss of life in 1939 and again in 1960, when nearly 200 miles of coastline in the center of the country sank six feet into the Pacific.

The high mountains and exceptionally clear atmosphere have also brought two different kinds of communities to the northern regions. As the *norte grande* gives way to the more fertile *norte chico* or "small north" in places like the Elqui valley, there is the scientific community around the giant Tololo telescope. Many foreign scientists come here to gaze at the heavens as the clear skies offer perfect visibility for over half the year. Also gazing up at the heavens are the members of many alternative communities who have set up in the Elqui valley and other nearby spots, to practice different kinds of oriental religion and meditation: a little piece of California in the heart of the Andes.

The Central Valley

As one travels south, the landscape gradually mellows, waters from the mountains make the land fertile, and the climate encourages agriculture, especially in the Central Valley, which makes up the third and fourth of the administrative regions. This is where most of the booming Chilean wine industry is located, as well as the huge orchards for apples and other soft fruits. It is also where the capital Santiago and the main port of Valparaíso are situated, and where the main passes across the Andes to Argentina can be found.

Founded by Pedro de Valdivia in 1541, Santiago, which occupies a separate unnumbered metropolitan region, lies in a beautiful site, with the tall mountains of the Andes in view, and surrounded by fertile wheat fields and orchards. In the mid-eighteenth century it made a fine sight, described by the English sailor John Byron:

> The city is very well pavemented; its gardens are full of orange trees and all kinds of flowers, which spread their perfume inside the houses and out into the streets. In the centre of the city lies the Plaza Real or royal square, with eight fine avenues leading up to it. On the western side of the square are the cathedral and the bishop's palace; to the north, the presidential palace, the royal court, the town council building and the prison; to the south are a whole line of arches occupied by a series of small shops, above which is a gallery where spectators gather to watch bullfights.

Little of this elegant and rational planning has survived in the modern city, which, with more than four million inhabitants, is the fifth largest in South America. Much of Chile's industry is also concentrated around the capital. This, combined with its location in a valley, produces grave problems of pollution and the phenomenon of thermal inversion, in which a layer of cold air lies over the city like a blanket, trapping the smog produced for days like a vast ugly pall. Schools are often closed in winter and the use of cars and buses is restricted. Even so, it is possible to escape from Santiago by traveling only a few miles, either down to the sea coast at resorts from La Serena down to Viña del Mar, or up into the mountains via the valley of the river Maipó.

The Central Valley continues down past Concepción, ending at the port of Puerto Montt at a latitude of more than 40 degrees south. For several centuries when Chile was governed by the Spanish, it was the city of Concepción on the river Bío-Bío which was considered the southern boundary of Chile, as the European settlers only managed to subdue the local indigenous population further south late in the nineteenth century.

The Opera House, Santiago

The South

Below Puerto Montt, the coastline becomes much more fragmented and is cut by steeply-sided valleys like the Norwegian fjords. Because the area was settled by Europeans at the end of the nineteenth century or early in the twentieth, some of the towns have a distinctly German or Alpine atmosphere, although the magnificent cones of volcanoes such as Mount Osorno clearly mark the difference with Europe. It is here that the vast forests also begin, in which traditional pines such as the *araucaria* (monkey puzzle tree) or *alerce* (larch) are increasingly giving way to managed tree plantations used for industrial purposes. Another very tangible sign of how humanity has started to modify nature comes in the tracts of bright yellow gorse which, as in New Zealand, tend to replace the native undergrowth. The first bushes were brought by European settlers in order to attract the bees used to produce honey, but now the gorse threatens to take over from all indigenous species, making the landscape even more "European." Even so, much of the countryside is breathtakingly beautiful, and is safeguarded in many national parks. The Pan-American highway ends at Puerto Montt, but one of the creations of the Pinochet era was the

Carretera Austral, the southern highway which has opened up much of this area for tourists and timber companies alike.

By the XI region, starting in the north at 45 degrees south at the town of Puerto Aisén and the regional capital Coihaique, there are few visitors or local inhabitants. Although the territory from here down to the south of Tierra del Fuego makes up one third of Chile, the population density is no more than one or two people per square mile. This is also true of the final, XII region, also known as Magellanes because it stretches down to the Magellan straits between the mainland of Latin America and Tierra del Fuego. Discovered for Europe by Ferdinand Magellan on his round-the-world voyage in 1520, the straits themselves have attracted continuing interest because of their strategic importance. The Spanish founded two settlements there in 1583, but all the pioneers died except for one, who was eventually rescued by a British ship. Several centuries later, in 1843, the straits were formally claimed for Chile by sailors from the island of Chiloé, who arrived just before a French vessel which intended to do the same for France.

At the very tip of the mainland lies the town of Punta Arenas, founded in 1848, and used for many years as a penal colony. In the latter part of the nineteenth century, it became an important port of call for ships rounding the continent and a thriving center for the wool industry. Records show that in 1906, for example, over ten million pounds of wool were exported to Britain alone. This was a golden age for the town, which could boast electric street lighting by 1896, almost fifteen years ahead of the country's capital. The boom was soon brought to an end by the opening of the Panama Canal in 1914 which offered ships a far quicker route between the continent's west and east coasts, but the town's strategic importance was re-affirmed in 1982 during the conflict between Argentina and Britain over the Falklands/Malvinas islands, when Punta Arenas became a key logistical base for the British forces.

Tierra del Fuego itself is split in a vertical north-south division with Argentina, and although often thought of as one main island, is in fact an archipelago of over a thousand islands. The Chileans have the southernmost town in the world on Isla Navarino at Puerto Williams, named after the British captain of the ship who claimed the land for Chile. The question of territorial rights with Argentina has not always been cordial, and in the 1970s the two nations almost clashed when the Queen of England (appointed arbitrator by both countries for historical reasons) awarded the three small islands of Lennox, Picton, and Nueva to Argentina. Chile appealed to the Pope, but he confirmed the judgment, a ruling accepted only with extreme bad grace by the then military government in Santiago. With the possibility of oil deposits in the area, there is still considerable

Moais on Easter Island

David Horwell/South American Pictures

tension between the two countries over the exact line of demarcation, as there is further up on the mainland.

Chile also lays claim to a large section of Antarctica. It maintains a permanent scientific base at Teniente Marsh, and consistently supports the argument that the continent should be governed solely by South American countries, rather than Europeans or other countries who also have bases there. Perhaps the most spectacular affirmation of Chile as an Antarctic power was when an iceberg was towed from there and sent to the world fair in Seville in Spain in 1992.

Easter Island

This small island, the Isla de Pascua or Rapa Nui, stands almost 2,500 miles out in the Pacific Ocean and has been administered by Chile since 1888. It is famous above all for the hundreds of *moai*, the carved stone statues of human heads and torsos which dot the island. What makes them so mysterious is that they were obviously produced and installed by a civilization with a high degree of artistic and technical expertise, but which has left no discernible traces among today's inhabitants. Various experts have speculated on how this may have happened: the Norwegian anthropologist Thor Heyerdahl was convinced that the island must have been populated by people from the Polynesian islands much further to the

An Easter islander   *Julio Etchart/Reportage*

west. In the late 1940s he sailed his wooden raft, *Kon Tiki*, from mainland South America across the Pacific, to prove that contact between the two cultures was possible. On Easter Island, he again used primitive tools he thought could have been used by earlier peoples to raise the huge statues, some of which weigh over twenty tons. According to Heyerdahl, no knowledge of how or why they were erected had been passed down because there had been a war between two groups which ended with a massacre and the flight of the victors.

A further mystery are the wooden tablets or *rongo-rongo*, covered with tiny pictures, whose meaning has never been convincingly deciphered. The intricate texts are now thought to have been "creation songs," written in response to the first attempts by missionaries to explain the Christian view of creation to the islanders.

What is known is that the Easter Islanders suffered terribly from their contact with South American and European civilization. In the mid-nineteenth century, most of them were taken to Peru to work as virtual slaves. After an international campaign, fifteen survivors were eventually returned to the island, but they caused havoc among the remaining 5,000 inhabitants by importing infectious diseases which wiped out almost 80 per cent of the population. The islanders' situation hardly improved after they became part of Chile; in 1934 a visiting anthropologist wrote of their desperate state: "Due to neglect by the Chileans, or even worse, due to the harmful influence of the people sent out there, the island has not so much fallen into decay as rotted away, in the midst of hopeless misery."

In recent years, thanks to income from tourism and a more enlightened approach from the Chilean authorities, the islanders' way of life has improved. It was, however, one of the wilder schemes of the Pinochet government to allow Easter Island to be used as an emergency landing site for U.S. space shuttle craft.

Crusoe's Island

The Juan Fernández Islands, 400 miles out in the Pacific and halfway down the coast of Chile, owe their fame to literature. Six hundred people, with two cars between them, live on the main island, called Robinson Crusoe after Daniel Defoe's celebrated novel. Although Defoe situated his tale in the Caribbean, it was in fact on Juan Fernández that the Scottish sailor Alexander Selkirk was put ashore in 1704, after he had argued with the captain of a pirate ship which he was supposed to be accompanying on a round-the-world voyage. Selkirk lived on the island, with no Man Friday, for four years and four months, until he was rescued and returned to Bristol. His experiences obviously made it hard for him to settle, and after drifting from town to town in England and Scotland, he eventually put to sea again and died during the journey. Nowadays, the tourists who brave the flight or the 36-hour boat crossing are shown the cave where he lived on the beach, and the vantage point high on the mountain in the middle of the island from which he kept a lookout for any passing ship.

Chiloé

In *What Am I Doing Here?*, Bruce Chatwin wrote, "The island of Chiloé is celebrated for its black storms and black soil, its thickets of fuchsia and bamboo, its Jesuit churches and the golden hands of its woodcarvers." Chiloé is the place where Chile's most traditional way of life continues to thrive. Although it is only half an hour by ferry from the port of Puerto Montt on the mainland, the island seems to be from another time altogether. In part this is due to a continuing sense of isolation, which started during Spanish colonization; in part due to the strong influence of the Jesuits, who helped the local population to plant and farm the land in a self-sufficient way; and in part due to almost everything, as Bruce Chatwin observed, being made from wood. The *Chilotes*, as the inhabitants of the island are called, have always seen themselves as distinct from the mainlanders. They did not want independence from Spain, and before finally becoming part of independent Chile in 1826, offered to become subjects of the British Crown. Nowadays, most islanders live from fishing and salmon and lobster farming.

Peoples of Chile

Chile's natural barriers meant that it was one of the last regions in Latin America to be populated. Archaeological remains from about 14,000 years ago include traces of pots and the bones of mastodons which had been hunted and eaten. These early settlements were on the northern coastline, and for thousands of years the first Chileans seem to have lived in small groups on the coast or in the fertile river valleys. Closer to our own times, remains of their villages have been found, together with evidence that these indigenous peoples raised llamas for wool and milk. The northern groups gradually came into the orbit of the highland peoples of Bolivia and Peru, the civilizations of Tiahuanaco and the Incas. Like them, they spoke the Aymara language and lived a harsh life, based on the cultivation of crops such as corn and potatoes. The Incas conquered the northern half of Chile only a couple of generations before the Spanish arrived, so there were no great population centers or developed sites in Chile. Today, the Aymara number only around 40,000 people, and like their ancestors live mainly from tending herds of goats or llamas.

The Mapuche

Far more important numerically and in the history of Chile were the Araucanian Indians of the Central Valley and the southern highlands. Before the arrival of the Spanish there were probably more than half a million of them, usually divided into three groups: the Picunche, the most northerly group, the Mapuche, most numerous and powerful, and the Huilliche. They too were mostly farmers or nomadic hunters, living in groups of no more than a few hundred. But unlike their northern counterparts, the Mapuche were successful in joining together to defend their lands and way of life against the Spanish; the first conqueror of Chile, Pedro de Valdivia, met his death at their hands in 1554. From then until the final pacification of the Mapuche in 1880, there were periods of wars and uncertain truces as the two cultures coexisted uneasily.

After the Mapuche had finally made their peace, they found their lands, which they owned communally and to which they had no official titles, gradually invaded by European settlers. In the course of the last century, their territories have been reduced further and further, and even though they sought to have their ownership recognized by governments in the 1960s and early 1970s, they continue to be persecuted and forced off traditional lands. In 1997 the Mapuche and the national government clashed over plans to build a hydroelectric plant on the river Bío-Bío. According to the government, the scheme is essential to meet Chile's energy needs; the Mapuche see it as another way of forcing them off their lands and exploiting their traditional sites without consultation or compensation.

The Mapuche still number several hundred thousand, but face problems created by the increasing division of their land and the inadequacy of subsistence farming techniques, as well as the constant emigration of the young to the towns and cities in search of a more stable livelihood. In recent years however, the Mapuche have been organizing to preserve their language and their traditions, which still succeed in rallying their communities. There is a new generation of women *machis* or traditional healers and the game of *chueca* or hockey has been revived, as have many of the main ceremonies like the *ñgillatun,* the great festival of crops and fertility.

When the Mapuche seek to encourage the gods to bring them a good harvest, or want to give thanks for plentiful crops, they call all the families of a reservation together for the three-day *ñgillatun* celebration. The people in charge of the ceremony choose an empty field, and altars or *rewe* are set up. On the first day of the ceremony, the field is swept clean of evil spirits by four horsemen, who ride in circles, whooping and shouting, waving blue and white flags. By the altar, the chosen priest says a lengthy prayer to Ngenenchen the god creator, while all the guests dance in lines around him. Then an animal, usually a goat or ox, is ritually sacrificed. Its heart is plunged into the altar fire, its blood sprinkled on the ground and the flames, to purify and give thanks. The Mapuche dance and sing again around the altar, before retiring to their *ramada*, the temporary wooden shelter where each family receives its guests. Here they invite people to eat and drink chicha beer made from apples, native strawberries, or other fruit. Similar celebrations go on for three days, with every care taken to ensure that the traditional ceremonial is followed down to the last detail. Mapuches come from great distances to take part in these *ñgillatun*, which serve to impart a sense of community and belonging.

"Savages" of the South

Araucano Indian from a 19th c. drawing

The fate of the indigenous population in the far south of the mainland and on the islands of Tierra del Fuego is even more tragic. The scattered groups living on the Chilean coastline were left virtually untouched by the many years of Spanish rule, and it was only in the nineteenth century that the outside world began to impinge on them. At first this merely took the form of increasingly curious sea travelers, one of the most famous of whom was Charles Darwin, botanist on the HMS *Beagle* during its round-the-world voyage in the 1830s. His opinion of the indigenous groups he encountered on Tierra del Fuego was typical of the dismissive European view of such "savages":

December 17th, 1832 ... When we came within hail, one of the four natives who were present advanced to receive us, and began to shout most vehemently, wishing to direct us where to land. When we were on shore, the party looked rather alarmed, but continued talking and making gestures with great rapidity. It was without exception the most curious and interesting spectacle I ever beheld: I could not have believed how wide was the difference between savage and civilized man: it is greater than that between a wild and domesticated animal, inasmuch as in man there is a greater power of improvement ...

It was only at the start of the twentieth century that pressure on land began to affect the local populations even in these remote areas. Disturbing photographs from as recently as the 1920s show shooting parties out hunting Indians in order to clear them off the land for settlers. The hunters were paid a bounty for every pair of ears they brought in as proof of their kills. A respected author from one of Chile's most traditional families, Agustín Edwards, could write in *Peoples of Old* in 1924 of the Alacalufe Indians living in the far south: "They are human amphibians who are still living in a state of complete degradation and savagery, and have up to the present resisted all attempts to educate and civilize them."

Unfortunately, they were less successful at resisting disease or efforts by missionaries and others to put them into reservations. Of the indigenous groups from Tierra del Fuego, the Yaghans, the Onas, and the Alacalufe, only a last handful of the Alacalufe survive today.

Jemmy Buttons

Charles Darwin was not the only passenger on the *Beagle*. Perhaps the strangest guests were three young Indians from Tierra del Fuego. The captain of the ship, Robert Fitzroy, had picked up Jemmy Buttons, Fuegia Basket, and York Minster on a voyage three years earlier. He had taken them off to England, convinced that a good progressive English education would catapult them out of their backwardness. They were presented at Court and sent to good schools to learn English and all the social graces. On the voyage of the *Beagle* in 1832, Fitzroy wanted to return the three young people to their native land, together with an English missionary, so that the four of them could convert the other natives. When the *Beagle* arrived in the Straits of Magellan, the ship's party set up camp, dug a vegetable garden, and left the four of them on shore while they sailed off to explore further. On their return after only a week, the camp had been wrecked, Fuegia and York Minster did not even acknowledge them, and the terrified young missionary asked to be rescued at once. He was taken on board, but the three Indian youngsters were left behind, with the task of continuing to educate the others. When Fitzroy and the *Beagle* returned a year later, only Jemmy Buttons was left. Darwin wrote of him: "We could hardly recognize poor Jemmy. Instead of the clean, well-dressed stout lad we left him, we found him a naked thin squalid savage." Jemmy wanted nothing more to do with the Englishmen and returned to his previous way of life, apparently with no regrets.

Mixed Heritage

Most Chileans today have a very ambiguous attitude to their country's Indian heritage. On the one hand, indigenous culture is often celebrated for rhetorical purposes, as when in 1970, for example, President Salvador Allende quoted the sixteenth-century rebel Mapuche leader Lautaro in his inauguration speech. On the other, neglect and mistreatment still abound, and most Chileans continue to regard indigenous people as inferior. The fact is, however, that around 70 per cent of today's Chileans are mixed-race mestizos, with at least some indigenous ancestry. The Spaniards who first colonized the country in the sixteenth century were nearly all males, believing Chile to be dangerous frontier territory, and this led to many mixed marriages and many more children born out of wedlock. One of the notorious early exponents of such population growth was Francisco de Aguirre, the conqueror of the *norte grande*. When criticized by the Church for having fathered over 50 illegitimate children, he declared it must be rendering more of a service to God to create so many potential Christians than it was a sin.

Because Chile had neither great plantations nor intensive mining during colonial times, the number of blacks brought into the country from Africa as slaves was very small. One estimate in the early seventeenth century put their number at around 20,000, but these were gradually absorbed into the rest of the population, so that in common with Argentina, Chile today lacks any significant black culture.

European Migration

It was in the nineteenth century, after independence from Spain, that immigrants from other European countries began to arrive in Chile. French, Swiss, British, and, most significantly, German settlers headed to the south of the country and put their stamp on it: Valdivia, for example, is an almost German city, with its own German newspaper, and Osorno has a strongly German flavor. This was not the massive immigration as seen in Argentina, however, and numbered 200,000 at most. Between 1880 and 1900 Serbs and Croats settled in the far south, many hoping to find gold. Although these new colonists managed to find land in the extreme south, the richest region of the Central Valley had been in the hands of a few owners since Spanish times, and as the population grew, the newcomers largely settled in towns and cities, so that today over 80 per cent of Chileans are urban dwellers.

According to the last census in 1992, there are now almost fourteen million Chileans. Forty per cent are under 21 years old, but in recent years the birth rate has slowed to almost European levels, suggesting that Chile will experience only moderate growth into the next century.

Huasos, dressed for a rodeo — *Julio Etchart/Reportage*

Chilean Cowboys

Chileans may be overwhelmingly urbanized, but the country still has its own Wild West, and cowboys, known as *huasos,* still work on ranches and at the cattle markets of Osorno and Temuco. They are less numerous and less symbolic of national identity than Argentina's mythical *gauchos,* but nonetheless appeal to city-dwellers as romantic outsiders. In his book *Lost Cowboys,* the renowned gynecologist and yodeller Hank Wangford describes the intricacy of the *huaso* wardrobe:

> Chile's history is written on the huasos' legs. Given the intransigence of the Mapuche and the lack of integration by the conquerors, it is easy to see why the huasos stayed among their own. There are not the wide open spaces, the pampas, in Chile as in Argentina. Huasos did not develop as the gauchos did. They didn't disappear into the high pampas grass and hunt wild cattle, killing when they were hungry. They didn't interbreed as much with the Indians, or learn native ways like the gauchos. They remained outsiders, more like the north American Anglo cowboys. Their leggings reflect their colonial Spanish roots much more clearly than any of the gauchos' paraphernalia which, like their whole way of life, was far more Indian.
>
> Even so, the *huasos* still like to dress up. As well as their impressive leggings, they have three kinds of poncho. There is the poncho itself, the largest and a working garment, the *chamanto,* medium-sized and dressy, and the manta that I had seen at the rodeo … They wear a bolero-style *chaqueta* or jacket over the *chaleco,* waistcoat. Like the gauchos, they have a *faja* or belt and *panuelo* or bandana. Like the old Spanish, they have *manguillas* or cuffs. They don't carry a long-bladed *facón* stuck into the back of their belt but wear one piece of machismo that eclipses even the gauchos. Their spurs, *espuelas,* are gigantic.

2   HISTORY AND POLITICS: DEMOCRATS AND DICTATORS

The Independence Struggle

The Chile which won independence from Spain at the start of the nineteenth century was a country of less than a million inhabitants. It had little industry or mining, and was geographically the furthest colony from the motherland apart from the Philippines. Such wealth as it possessed came from the land, from wheat, tallow, and hides. Land ownership was dominated by the big estates given as a reward to Spanish soldiers who had fought to win the territory and then defend it against the Araucanians, the southern indigenous peoples who still controlled the country south of Concepción. The boundary with Argentina beyond the Andes was undefined in many areas, while in the north, Chilean territory ended below the Atacama desert. Its northern neighbor, Peru, was far wealthier and far more important to the Spanish empire; Chile was governed from Lima throughout colonial times.

As in the other Spanish possessions, it was Napoleon's invasion of Spain in 1808 which prompted the locally-born or *criollo* liberals in Santiago to think that they could throw off colonial rule. A local junta was formed at the end of 1810, but the Congress established soon after formulated a constitution in 1812 which still swore loyalty to the Spanish monarch. Nevertheless, the viceroy in Peru was concerned that the liberals would want more freedoms and sent a force to the island of Chiloé and Valdivia to re-conquer Chile. After the defeat of the young nationalist general Bernardo O'Higgins at Rancagua, the *reconquista* was complete and colonial status was re-imposed.

O'Higgins and other patriots crossed into Argentina to regroup. From there in 1817, they accompanied the Argentine general José de San Martín in his famous crossing of the high Andes with an army of 4,000 men. Chileans and Argentines defeated the royalist forces at the battle of Maipú; Chilean independence was officially declared on February 12, 1818.

Bernardo O'Higgins

Bernardo O'Higgins was the illegitimate son of an Irishman from Ballinary in Sligo, who had arrived in Peru in 1756 and risen in the service of the Spanish Crown to become Captain-General of Chile and Viceroy of Peru. Because of his florid Irish looks, his father was known to everyone as *el camarón:* the shrimp. Bernardo was born to Isabel Riquelme when his father was over 60, and the Viceroy never officially recognized his son until he was on his deathbed. Sent to England to gain an education,

Bernardo met up with Francisco de Miranda, who from London was busy plotting with everyone he could find to wrest Latin America from Spain. On his father's death, Bernardo returned to Chile to run a 64,000-acre estate in the south. From the start of the revolt against Spain, he played a leading role as a military commander. After defeat in 1814, he made his way across the Andes into exile in the city of Mendoza in Argentina. It was from there that he returned triumphantly alongside General San Martín, to defeat the royalist forces at Maipú. When the Argentine general refused any political position in the newly-liberated Chile, it was Bernardo O' Higgins who was named *Director Supremo*. After a further and decisive defeat of Spanish troops at Maipú in 1818, O'Higgins set about organizing the conquest of Peru. On this occasion, his chief ally was Lord Thomas Cochrane, a British naval commander who had become surplus to requirements in Britain after the defeat of Napoleon. Cochrane took the last remaining royalist stronghold in mainland Chile at Valdivia, and helped ship the newly-formed Chilean army up to Peru. O'Higgins himself remained an autocratic ruler of Chile until 1823 (saying of the poor "if they will not become happy by their own efforts, they shall be made happy by force. By God! They shall be happy!"). That year he was deposed by a coup led by the Catholic Church, elements of the old aristocracy, and provincial interests. A British ship took him into exile in Peru, accompanied by his mother, sister, and a parrot trained to say "my son, the *Director Supremo.*" He died in Lima in 1842.

O'Higgins became the republic's first president. After some years of political instability, the national constitution of 1833 was promulgated, which in the nineteenth century was responsible for ushering in a period of several decades during which civilian presidents followed one another at ten-yearly intervals. This stability was in sharp contrast to the difficulties which Argentina and many other of the emerging republics found in achieving a settled political system, and enabled Chile to develop its economy rapidly. Political power was still almost entirely in the hands of the owners of the large estates and businessmen in the growing cities.

War and Peace

Much of the economy was based on agriculture, but in the second half of the nineteenth century the desert north became crucially important for Chile. It was from the coasts here that the huge deposits of guano, or bird excrement, were dug and exported as fertilizer. Then the nitrates formed naturally in the deserts took the place of guano. In 1879, the Chilean government reacted violently to Bolivian attempts to tax nitrate mines run by Chileans in the province of Antofogasta. Peru took Bolivia's side, and

Bernardo O'Higgins   *Tony Morrison/South American Pictures*

so began the War of the Pacific which was to last until 1883. A fresh crop of national heroes was created, such as Captain Arturo Prat. Prat was defending the northern port of Iquique with two wooden ships when he came under attack by the iron-clad Peruvian warship *Huascar*. As his vessel was sunk under him, the gallant Prat leapt on board the Peruvian ship and fought on until he met his death. *Pratomania* swept through Chile, as the naval captain became a national symbol of bravery and sacrifice.

Chile eventually won the war on the battlefield; its troops entered Lima and forced Peru's surrender, while cutting Bolivia off from access to the Pacific Ocean. Victory was double-edged. To pay for the war, bonds on the nitrate mines were sold off cheaply, and most of these ended up in the hands of English speculators such as John North, who came to own a large part of the industry (see p. 42). But Chile had also conquered a huge amount of new territory, which has been the mainstay of its economy ever since. The war also helped to create the kind of nationalist ill-feeling between neighboring countries common throughout Latin America which continues to surface at moments of tension and often impedes political and economic integration.

In the south of Chile, the year 1880 saw the final truce with the Mapuche and other Araucanian groups. This signaled an expansion of colonization down beyond the 40th parallel, a move accelerated by the building of railways and the first reliable roads. Soon the Mapuche found that peace was even more of a threat to their territorial integrity than war.

One of the French settlers drawn to the south of Chile was the colorfully-named Orllie Antoine. Orllie's stroke of genius (or madness) was to exploit Mapuche mistrust of the Chilean state and to persuade them to make him their king. In 1860, he set off from Concepción with one servant and several mules. When he arrived among the Mapuche, his speeches about forming an independent nation to take on the Chileans were so convincing that several groups accepted him as their leader, and on November 17, 1860 he proclaimed himself Orllie-Antoine I, King of Araucania. His reign lasted only fourteen months. In January 1862 he was intercepted by a detachment of Chilean government troops, captured and sent up to Santiago. There he was tried, but declared insane. He was spared prison and instead put on a ship back to France. Orllie was undeterred. In order to raise funds to finance a return to his kingdom, he began to sell titles to imaginary lands in Araucania, creating a whole monarchy in exile. In 1869, he set off again, choosing this time to start from the Argentine side of the Andes. Once again, the indigenous tribes of the Patagonian pampas received him with enthusiasm, so that by 1870 he was, in theory at least, the ruler of a territory far larger than France itself. On this occasion, it seems that Orllie never even got as far as Chile, but fled back to Europe as soon as he heard there were troops out looking for him. He spent the last years until his death back in France, still trying to raise funds and volunteers to go out and reclaim the vast kingdom of "New France" beyond the seas.

Power Struggles

Expansion both north and south led to an export boom and increasing prosperity for some Chileans at least. It also led to a prolonged period of political instability during which the life of the country was marked by a struggle between presidents and Congress for who should wield more power, the gradual emergence of parties representing the new working class, and the involvement of the armed forces as political arbiters. One of the most interesting political experiments came under the presidency of José Manuel Balmaceda from 1886 to 1891. Balmaceda used the revenues from nitrate exports to create the modern Chilean state. In 1887 he set up a ministry of public works, building roads, railways, and other infrastructure throughout the country. He was opposed by the political interests represented by Congress, particularly the traditional Conservative and Liberal parties, and eventually in 1891 a civil war broke out. At least 6,000 people died in the fighting, in which the Chilean navy and the army found themselves on opposite sides, thus further confirming their role as political actors on the national scene.

After Balmaceda's downfall and eventual suicide, the rule of Congress and the political parties was strengthened. It was also during this period that the first trade unions were organized to defend workers' rights: more than 200 strikes occurred in the twenty years after 1890, as well as such violent incidents as the killing by troops of several hundred nitrate workers and their families in the school of Santa María in the northern port of Iquique in 1907. Thanks to the efforts of Luis Emilio Recabarren, and others, these unions evolved into political parties, with both the Socialist Party and the Communist Party of Chile being created by the early 1920s.

When a reforming president, Arturo Alessandri (the "lion of Tarapaca"), came to power in 1920, he promised constitutional and social reform to adapt the political system to changes in society, but failed to get many significant measures through a hostile Congress. It was when complete

Shipping nitrate at Pisagua, Chile, 1890s   *Illustrated London News*

stalemate was reached, in a worsening economic climate as Chile's natural nitrates lost their world markets to synthetic fertilizers first produced in Germany, that the Chilean armed forces stepped in. In September 1924 they deposed the president, and for the next year-and-a-half Congress was closed and either military juntas or Alessandri himself ruled by decree. Eventually in 1927 one of the military conspirators, Colonel Carlos Ibáñez, was elected president. He outlawed the Communist Party and independent trade unions, but used the increased presidential powers granted under a new national constitution passed in 1925 to bring in a fresh program of public works and stimulate industry.

The worldwide depression at the end of the 1920s brought about Ibáñez' downfall. The international price of copper plummeted, so that exports which had been worth $111 million fell to less than a third of that value. Street protests in 1931 led to Ibáñez' resignation and exile in Argentina. As the depression gripped Chile ever more tightly, 1932 saw the country proclaimed a "socialist republic" under the journalist Carlos Dávila and the charmingly-named Marmaduke Grove. The republic lasted only a hundred days; after a further military intervention Arturo Alessandri again found himself in the Moneda Palace.

Alessandri was to rule for six years until 1938. During this time, he helped bring Chile out of its economic decline, and breathed fresh life into the parliamentary parties. At the same time, he is remembered by many in

Chile for his harsh authoritarianism, and the vicious repression used at times to subdue workers and political opponents.

In 1938, a Popular Front government came to power. This came about thanks to an alliance between the Communist Party, the Radicals, and the Socialists, who all became convinced that only such a united front could keep Alessandri out of office. The challenge for it and subsequent administrations was to make the political system more responsive to the changing economic and social realities of the country, to help Chile evolve from a situation described in the following terms by the North American author George McBride in 1935:

> A New World country with the social organization of old Spain, a twentieth-century people still preserving a feudal society; a republic based on the equality of man, yet with a blue-blooded aristocracy and a servile class as distinctly separated as in any of the monarchies of the Old World. Throughout Chile's history this situation has existed. It is this social heritage that forms the background for the present-day problems of the Chilean people.

The Popular Front was able to do little to resolve these problems, and collapsed in 1941. The following years saw presidents from the Radical Party, Juan Antonio Ríos and in 1946, Gabriel González Videla. Videla come to power thanks to the support of the Communists, but this did not prevent him from banning the party in 1948 after a series of Communist-organized strikes had threatened his government. Then came the return of the dictator Carlos Ibáñez, this time elected to power, and the return also of the Alessandri family in the shape of Arturo's son, Jorge, who was president of a right-wing administration from 1958 to 1964.

Rise of the Christian Democrats

By 1964, the population had grown to over eight million (from a little over four million in the early 1930s). Already, more than three-quarters of this population were town dwellers. Many of them were working in the new industries that had been encouraged since the end of the 1930s, or were in the well-organized state service sector (a national health service was set up in 1952). After winning the vote in 1949, women also began to make an impact on the political scene. From 1957 onwards, many of these people turned to a new party, the Christian Democrats, to give voice to their concerns.

In the 1964 elections the Christian Democrat Eduardo Frei was chosen as president. He promised a "revolution in liberty" and a "communitarian society," a third way between what Frei described in a 1964 speech as "reactionaries with no conscience" and "revolutionaries with no brains."

The main planks of the Christian Democrat revolution were *promoción popular*, a sweeping agrarian reform, and a new approach to the copper industry. *Promoción popular* involved increasing expenditure on education and the creation of local self-help organizations, particularly among the newer neighborhoods of the rapidly expanding towns and cities. The agrarian reform, pushed through with a new law in 1967, authorized the expropriation of all farms over 180 acres in size, which were then administered by a committee of peasant representatives. To pay for this and other social reforms, Frei sought to gain more control over the copper industry, dominated by the U.S. firms of Kennecott and Anaconda. In what was called the "Chileanization" of the industry, the state took a 51 per cent holding in the companies.

Taken together, these moves represented the most far-reaching changes to Chilean society since the early 1930s. They also had the effect of sharply polarizing political opinion. On the left, new radical groups such as the Movement of the Revolutionary Left (MIR) founded in 1965 in the University of Concepción, or the left-wing Christian Democrat grouping, Movement for United Popular Action (MAPU), thought that the changes should be used as a springboard to push for a true revolution. The socialists and Communists also saw the Frei government's reforms as the first step towards more profound changes in Chilean society. On the right, the National Party (PN) condemned the growing social ferment and predicted chaos unless the reforms were reversed.

Popular Unity

Such was the tense political situation when the 1970 elections took place. The Christian Democrat hold on power had been weakened because of inflation and poor economic growth, while political enemies had gained in influence. The parties of the left (Socialists, Communists, and Radicals, together with MAPU and some other smaller groups) formed the *Unidad Popular* (Popular Unity) and put forward the veteran Socialist Salvador Allende as their candidate. The right stood behind former president Jorge Alessandri. In elections on September 4,1970, Salvador Allende emerged as the winner with the smallest of margins: some 40,000 votes out of three million.

Since none of the candidates had gained an absolute majority, Congress had to confirm Allende as president. The right-wing parties, planning an eventual military coup, embarked on a scare campaign which backfired badly on them when a group of officers attempted to kidnap the head of the army, General René Schneider, who was a convinced constitutionalist, and mortally wounded him. The outrage at this murder was so great that it tipped the balance in favor of Allende, who finally won the backing of Congress as president; *Viva Chile, mierda!* ("Long live Chile, shit!") was the triumphant cry of one Socialist deputy on hearing the result, a cry unfortunately broadcast live on radio across the country.

This was the 62-year-old Allende's fourth attempt to win the presidency. Although Popular Unity did not have a majority in either the Congress or the Senate, the government plunged into its radical program, designed to show the world "the Chilean road to socialism." There was a determined effort to redistribute national income in favor of the poorer classes, and the Allende government stepped up social spending on education, health, and housing. It embarked on a much more far-reaching process of agrarian reform, which was so effective that by the end of 1972, all rural properties over 200 acres in size had been split up. It declared "a second independence" in nationalizing major industrial concerns and buying out the foreign copper companies. In the case of the copper companies, no compensation was paid, as Allende considered that they owed Chile millions of dollars due to years of "excessive profits." The Chilean people found themselves involved in political life and difficult choices to an unprecedented extent.

Although the first year of the Popular Unity government was remarkably successful, by the end of 1971 the strains were beginning to show. The parties in the governing coalition were deeply divided on how quickly and how deeply to bring in change. President Allende was backed by the Radicals and the Communists in his attempts to control the process as carefully as possible.

But much of his own Socialist Party and the revolutionary left-wing groups such as MIR were constantly urging the government to quicken the pace of reform and to achieve a fully-fledged revolution as quickly as possible. To do this, they encouraged the peasants to take over estates without waiting for "bureaucratic decrees"; they also incited the workers to take over factories and "socialize production."

Destabilization

Outside the coalition, political opposition to the Allende government also hardened. The Christian Democrats, who had supported Allende's appointment and backed him on the nationalization of the copper mines, turned against the government over the accelerating pace of take-overs and, more particularly, when it tried to promote the Unified National School (ENU), with its educational goal of forming the *hombre nuevo*, the revolutionary hero "free to develop himself fully in a non-capitalist society." The National Party continued its noisy opposition, encouraging such anti-government demonstrations as the "march of the empty saucepans," staged by middle-class housewives in December 1971 when the Cuban president Fidel Castro was visiting Santiago, or the national truck owners' strike of the following year which did much to weaken the government by causing widespread shortages and pushing up inflation.

In addition to this domestic opposition, the U.S. companies and their allies in Washington did all they could to stifle Popular Unity's initiatives. The copper companies which had been expropriated fought the decision in international courts, creating uncertainty about the legality of the move. Before and during the 1970 election, the U.S. multinational telephone company ITT offered money to the CIA to help prevent Allende coming to power; after the elections, the agency spent some $8 million in attempts to destabilize the regime by financing opponents, supplying payments to the opposition press, and initiating a whole variety of "dirty tricks." As Secretary of State Henry Kissinger said after the 1973 coup which brought about Allende's downfall: "I don't see why we need to stand idly by and watch a country go communist due to the irresponsibility of its own people."

In addition, whether fortuitously or as the result of deliberate pressure, the price of Chile's essential export, copper, fell dramatically on international markets, thus making it even harder for the Allende government to pay for the ambitious program of social spending it envisaged.

The Military Coup

Then of course, there was the armed forces' hostility to the Allende administration. Almost from the start of the Unidad Popular, the National Party and others were calling on the military to intervene, but the generals held back. As tension mounted, the president tried to win them over by including General Carlos Prats and two other officers in his cabinet, but as the country became paralyzed by turmoil in 1973, they became increasingly restless. A June 1973 uprising by a tank regiment was personally quelled by Prats. The left-wing groups responded by taking over more factories around the capital, and demanding that Allende "arm the people" for the inevitable battle with the armed forces. Inflation was rampant; there were strikes and civil disorder in almost every sector of the economy; the truck drivers went on strike again, joined by many professionals; civil war seemed inevitable.

On August 21, 1973 Prats was replaced as minister of defense by General Augusto Pinochet. His immediate response came in the form of a military coup which started on the night of September 10-11, and by sunset on the following day President Allende lay dead in the ruins of the Moneda Palace, which had been bombarded by British-made Hawker Hunter jets and stormed by infantry units. In a last broadcast put out by a loyal radio station, President Allende spoke of his hopes for the future:

La Moneda under bomb attack

I have faith in Chile and in its destiny. Other men will overcome this dark and bitter moment, when treason strains to conquer. May you go forward in the knowledge that, sooner rather than later, the great avenues will open once again along which free citizens will march to build a better society. Long live Chile! Long live the people! Long live the workers! These are my last words, but I am sure my sacrifice will not be in vain. I am sure that this sacrifice will constitute a moral lesson that will punish cowardice, perfidy, and treason.

Torture and Exile

Although there had been several military interventions in Chilean political life, the September 11, 1973 coup was the most violent and the longest-lasting. Several hundred people were killed during the take-over itself, and thousands more died in the repression which followed. One example was the infamous trip to the north of Chile by General Arellano Stark in October 1973. From mass graves dug up in 1990 and other evidence, a diary of his visits to various towns was compiled: "On October 16, fifteen people executed in La Serena ... October 17 in Copiapo another 13; 19th: Antofogasta, 18 shot. That same afternoon, in Calama, 26 political prisoners were taken out and executed, all to show that the military regime meant business."

Most of the victims were members of the Socialist and Communist parties, the MIR or other left-wing groups; trade unionists, student leaders, and workers' representatives were also targets. More than 7,000 suspects were rounded up and put into the national Soccer stadium for interrogation; many were never seen or heard of again. When the body of left-wing musician Victor Jara was recovered from the morgue, it was discovered that the guitarist's hands had been broken during torture. The Chilean military, backed by the CIA, followed the example of their Guatemalan counterparts and simply made people "disappear," abducting, torturing, and murdering them without ever accepting any knowledge of their whereabouts. A secret police organization, known as the National

Armed forces on
Santiago's main streets

Directorate of Intelligence (DINA), was set up to carry out the repression, and struck down opponents outside Chile as well as at home. General Prats and his wife were blown up in Buenos Aires, while Allende's foreign minister, Orlando Letelier, was even assassinated in Washington, D.C.

Chilean society was torn apart. Thousands were thrown out of work because they had supported the previous regime. Political differences made enemies within families, between neighbors and workmates. Several hundred thousand Chileans went into foreign exile. The socialist experiment in Chile had attracted the attention of many people abroad, who had seen it as the second possibility, after the Cuban Revolution of 1959, for revolutionary ideals to take hold in Latin America. The exodus of Chileans from their country in the 1970s resembled what happened at the end of the Spanish Civil War. These new exiles helped bring an awareness of the political struggle going on in this remote corner of the globe, as they helped set up solidarity groups in many countries, and encouraged labor organizations throughout the world to boycott and isolate the military regime.

Within Chile itself, all political and trade union activity was banned. The media were brought under strict control, while military officers were drafted in to take over not only all the main industries, but the universities as well.

Pinochet's Chile

General Pinochet was soon the undisputed dictator of Chile. The other armed forces chiefs were members of the ruling junta, but clearly played a subordinate role. At one point, Pinochet even claimed that "there is not a leaf in Chile that stirs without me knowing it." Yet the economy which Pinochet had taken over after the three years of Popular Unity was in tatters. In September 1973 inflation had reached 900 per cent a year, there was a huge government deficit, basic goods were subject to shortages, and an estimated 600 state-run enterprises, employing five per cent of the workforce, were losing $500 million a year.

At first, the junta adopted a pragmatic series of measures, reducing the fiscal deficit and cutting state spending. The result was increased unemployment and a drop in the value of wages. Yet as Pinochet's hold on power tightened, he increasingly came under the influence of a group of economists who advocated much more radical economic reforms. They were known as the "Chicago Boys," since many of them had carried out postgraduate studies in that university, which was closely identified with the free-market economic ideas of Friedrich von Hayek and Milton Friedman, and rapidly came to dominate the military's economic policies. The main thrust of their brand of conservative "Reaganomics" was to reduce the role of the state in the national economy, and to promote private enterprise by opening up the economy to the rest of the world. In this neo-liberal blueprint, economic growth was to be achieved by increasing exports, while dramatically reducing the state sector and social spending. This effort was supported from Washington by the International Monetary Fund and the World Bank. Private banks in the U.S. and Europe used the abundant "petrodollars" which had flowed into their coffers in the wake of the first international oil crisis to finance the new economic groupings which emerged in Chile at this time.

The resulting "shock treatment" was a dose of bitter medicine. Public spending was cut by 27 per cent in 1975 and by 1979 had fallen to half its 1973 level. In an attempt to squeeze inflation out of the economy, the government opted for a fierce recession, and GDP shrank by thirteen per cent in 1976. The poor became poorer as purchasing power fell to 40 per cent of its 1970 level. Unemployment reached record levels. The extremism of the economic policy was recognized by junta member Admiral José Toribio Merino, who likened the economy to "a jungle of savage beasts, where he who can kill the one next to him, kills him."

By the late 1970s, these draconian reforms were meeting with some macro-economic success. As the world recession receded, the economy began to grow steadily, reaching average annual increases of 6.5 per cent. Inflation had fallen to 65 per cent by 1977, exports were booming and the balance-of-payments deficit was much reduced. With U.S. financial support and the systematic repression of political opposition, the "Chilean miracle" was underway.

Encouraged by his economic model, Pinochet now moved to insti-tutionalize his political model in a more permanent fashion. To do so, he had a new national constitution drawn up, which greatly weakened the power of political parties (excluding those which promoted "class struggle"), and provided for an eight-year presidency. To no one's surprise, Pinochet ap-pointed himself for the first eight-year period, from 1981-1989. At the end of this time, a plebiscite was to be held which could either accept the military candidate (Pinochet again, inevitably) or, if voters rejected this option, allow for presidential and congressional elections to be held. Pinochet also arranged for an amnesty to be passed which protected any members of the armed forces suspected of committing human rights abuses from prosecution.

Pinochet and his generals

The new constitution was approved by a large majority on September 11, 1980, the seventh anniversary of the coup. It seemed that Pinochet, like Franco in Spain before him, was seeking to remain in power forever. Increasing frustration at this, and the sudden collapse of the economic situation over the next two years, led to renewed protests and struggle from both the still banned political parties and the labor movement. A series of one-day strikes and protests shook the regime, which retaliated with more repression, using the murder of labor leaders, activists, and socially committed priests as a means of intimidation.

Opposition to Dictatorship

Beyond Chile too, the dictatorship was coming under fire. The Reagan administration abandoned its earlier support and indicated that it would prefer him to step down, fearful that further polarization would encourage a revival of the left. Pinochet himself narrowly survived an assassination attempt in 1986, allegedly supported by the CIA. Gradually the politicians realized that if they were to rid Chile of Pinochet, they would have to organize and fight back within the framework of the new constitution, however much they disagreed with it.

By February 1988 the main opposition parties, the Christian Democrats, the Socialists, and the Radicals, had worked out a common strategy. They presented this as the *Concertación de partidos por el NO* (the cross-party NO accord), aimed at rejecting the most crucial element of Pinochet's plan, his continuation in power after 1989. When the plebiscite took place on October 5, 1988, the "No" voters were triumphant, winning 54 per cent, but still, 43 per cent voted for eight more years of Pinochet.

The general was not amused at the result, famously comparing it to the biblical choice of Barabbas over Jesus. But he was caught in a trap of his own making, and now had to follow the other option outlined in the 1980 constitution: the holding of elections for a new president and Congress.

Evolving into an electoral alliance, the Concertación worked together again to win these, and in December 1989, the Christian Democrat leader Patricio Aylwin became the first elected president of Chile in almost twenty years. According to the new constitution, however, Pinochet was to remain commander-in-chief until 1998.

General Pinochet

General Pinochet's dictatorship from 1973 to 1989 was the longest uninterrupted period in power enjoyed by any Chilean since the arrival of the Spanish in 1540. Many Chileans see him as no more than a butcher in uniform, but others would agree with his own assessment that he defeated communism in Chile and should be congratulated for it.

Pinochet was born in the seaport of Valparaíso on November 25, 1915, the son of a customs agent and a domineering mother. Critics say that this was the origin of a life-long psychological trait: submission to ambitious women, who helped him make up his mind and stiffen his resolve. As in many lower middle-class families, his mother saw a military career as a way to social advancement, and after graduating from military college, the young Lieutenant Pinochet further helped himself up the social ladder by marrying the daughter of a former president, Lucia Hiriart, from one of Chile's "aristocratic" families. Pinochet steadily advanced as an officer and instructor at the military academy, and by the time Salvador Allende was elected president, he was already a general.

The fact that Pinochet had never expressed any political opinions in his already lengthy career led the Socialist president to trust him, and he was appointed army commander in 1972. It is still hotly debated whether or not he was one of the main instigators of the September 1973 coup which overthrew Allende's government. What is less in doubt is the fact that he immediately took the lead in the military junta, and became the driving force behind the savage repression which followed. Pinochet has always argued that this was the only way to "defeat communism" in Chile. To do so, he closed parliament, banned political parties and trade unions, hunted down left-wing groups and their sympathizers, and condoned torture and murder as instruments of his policies.

His image in those years became infamous. A small man with a high-pitched, grating voice, he boasted a spotless uniform and often added to his sinister appearance by wearing dark glasses. When he felt under attack, as he usually did from foreign journalists, his protruding teeth and shifty look made him seem like a wild boar at bay. He apparently could never understand the hatred he provoked and was extremely bitter that he was shunned internationally as a ruthless dictator. Although vain and ambitious, it seems that his innate disdain for politicians prevented him from encouraging a political movement to grow up around him, as had been the case with one of his avowed heroes, General Franco. Like many dictators, he is reported to be charming and affable when at home, and kind to animals and children.

CHILE

With its long and varied Pacific coastline, Chile is a country dominated by the sea. Fishing is an important part of the economy, but a rugged coastal geography means that there are few ports.

Stunning scenery - the snow-capped peak of Torre del Paine, national park, southern Chile.
(Tony Morrison/South American Pictures)

The fjord district: harbor at Puerto Aguirre
(Sue Mann/South American Pictures)

The market in Castro, island of Chiloé
(Sue Mann/South American Pictures)

EARNING A LIVING FROM THE SEA

Sea coalers, salvaging coal from the ocean, Lota, southern Chile
(Julio Etchart/Reportage)

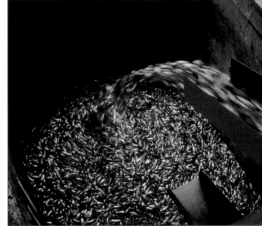

Seafood caught in southern
Chile and a fishmeal factory
(Julio Etchart/Reportage)

The fishing fleet at Puerto Montt
(Julio Etchart/Reportage)

Wood-chip mountains for export to
Japan, Concepción
(Julio Etchart/Reportage)

Tourists in Antartica
Peter Dixon (South American Pictures)

The view over the Atacama desert from the European Southern Observatory
(Hugh O'Shaughnessy)

The Atacama desert coast and guano-covered "La Portada rocks"
(Jason P Howe/South American Pictures)

Villarrica volcano
(Robert Francis/South American Pictures)

At a rally for the first free democratic elections in 16 years.

Julio Etchart/Reportage

Return to Democracy

President Aylwin was always careful to speak of his four years in power as the "transition to democracy." He was skillful in managing the legacy of seventeen years of military rule, so that in 1993 the Chilean deputy secretary-general of Amnesty International, José Zalaquett, could say, "Chile is now widely seen as the country in transition from dictatorship where social peace has been achieved most completely and most rapidly."

One of the first measures the new civilian government took to achieve this was to set up a "National Commission for Truth and Reconciliation" under former senator Raúl Rettig. The Rettig report was published in March 1991, and detailed more than 3,000 deaths committed by the security forces during and after the 1973 coup, as well as many thousands of cases of torture and other human rights abuses. Despite the overwhelming evidence of this report, Aylwin refused to put Pinochet and the other military leaders on trial, as had happened in neighboring Argentina. Many Chileans criticized what they saw as military impunity. Others argued that the government had no choice but to recognize that the military authorities had passed their own amnesty law in 1978 and that Pinochet was still commander-in-chief and quite capable of disrupting constitutional rule again if he thought that civilians were attacking the armed forces.

As a result, prosecutions for human right abuses were largely left to individuals, who met with little success in their efforts to find justice. This was in part because many members of the judiciary, and in particular the supreme court judges, were people who had been appointed during the military dictatorship.

Pinochet, as chief
of the army

Julio Etchart/
Reportage

Another step towards reconciliation in Chilean society was the effort made to welcome back the hundreds of thousands of Chileans who had been forced into exile. The return to Chile was often painful for people who had built another life abroad. Some of those who returned considered all those who had stayed as "collaborators," while many Chileans who had suffered the effects of the dictatorship day after day saw the returning exiles as "cowards" who had run away. To his credit, Aylwin used his four years in power to smooth over these differences. He also released all but two of the hundreds of political prisoners still held in jail, including those responsible for the assassination attempt on General Pinochet.

Political violence was remarkably rare during Aylwin's term of office, partly because all the major parties shared a broadly consensual view of Chile's economic direction. Political and party differences had also lost much of their edge during the Pinochet decade. Congress itself had been removed from the capital and was now installed in a monstrous modern building in Valparaíso in what was another gesture of Pinochet's contempt for politicians. The new constitution also weakened the position of the political parties, so that President Aylwin often ruled by decree, although his room for maneuver was blocked by the senators appointed by the outgoing military regime. These senators had been written into the constitution as part of Pinochet's efforts to achieve an in-built right-wing bias in Congress.

The parties of the Concertación continued to work together after the 1990 elections. The Christian Democrats were the senior members of the coalition, but unlike in the 1960s or early 1970s, they accepted the compromise of working with the Socialists, now very much a non-Marxist party of the moderate center, and other parties of the left. Thanks to continued economic growth and controlled inflation, the Aylwin government was able to increase social spending in health and education, but there were no radical new initiatives.

Culture of Consensus

Cooperation between the Concertación parties continued into the presidential elections at the end of 1993, when Eduardo Frei, the Christian Democrat son of the 1960s president, was chosen as their candidate. The right-wing vote was split between National Renovation and the Independent

President Eduardo Frei   *Julio Etchart/Reportage*

Democratic Union, which often seemed to be fighting each other rather than the other parties.

In December 1993, Eduardo Frei was elected as president with a large majority. His period in office is due to last six years, until the end of the century. The lackluster campaign showed that after years of polarization, the voters and political parties were much more interested in finding a consensus and working out pragmatic compromises than in the clash of ideologies. Since his election, Frei has continued with the liberal, free-market policies which have brought Chile sustained growth since the mid1980s.

What political debate there has been has revolved around social issues: the introduction of divorce and the rejection of legalized abortion; environmental issues (the environmental candidate polled more votes than the Communist in the 1993 elections); and the need to do more to help ease sharp social inequalities in housing, education, health, and welfare, which are the legacy of the Pinochet regime.

Two important events will mark Chile's immediate political future. In 1998 General Pinochet finally steps down as commander-in-chief of the army. The following year, there will be another presidential election. Will the Socialist Party, after having supported two Christian Democrat candidates, insist that it is their turn? And will the new generation of Chileans who vote in that election consider that the lessons of the past have been learned, and that socialism in Chile need not end in chaos and military intervention?

3   THE ECONOMY: LATIN AMERICA'S MIRACLE?

Seventeen hours a day, the giant 180-ton trucks clamber round and round the gouged out sides of the world's largest open-cast copper mine at Chuquicamata. Guided by computer, the monster trucks carry the ore up and out of the mine for shipment abroad. Chuquicamata is 14,000 feet up in the north Chilean Andes, one of a series of huge mines which contain no less than a fifth of all the world's copper reserves. Even gold and silver deposits here are merely a by-product of copper mining. The export of copper has been Chile's lifeline since the 1940s, when it replaced nitrates as the main earner of foreign currency. Nationalized under the Allende government, even General Pinochet kept the copper industry and the state company, CODELCO, out of his plans to privatize state concerns, perhaps because the armed forces made a stipulation in the 1980 constitution that ten per cent of revenues from the copper industry revenues should go directly to the military budget. CODELCO, the world's single largest copper producer, still operates Chuquicamata and several other enormous mines, and controls most of the country's deposits.

In the 1990s, however, foreign companies have been moving into the copper industry. The latest mines at Zaldivar or La Escondida now ship ore directly to the coast for loading onto ships through pipelines which start 10,000 feet up in the Andes. These new mines are run by Australian, Canadian, Finnish, or other multinational companies, attracted to Chile, according to one of their brochures, by "the good grades (of ore), less strict environmental controls, and labor costs." La Escondida is owned by a consortium made up of the U.S. Utah International company, the British Rio Tinto Zinc, and Japan's Mitsubishi Corporation and Nippon Mining Company. The activities of these new companies have considerably boosted copper production, but have already created conflict with environmentalists and more particularly with the fishermen of the northern coast, who fear that their industry, also vital to Chile's future, will be adversely affected by the constant activity on the coast.

Multinational involvement in the copper sector has also provoked anger among the trade unions, which are fighting the reduction in numbers and casualization of the labor force in an industry which has traditionally been well-organized and socially responsible. CODELCO still directly employs some 25,000 people and provides between ten and twenty per cent of government revenue, making it vitally important to the whole

Chuquicamata   *Julio Etchart/Reportage*

economy. To the foreign companies, however, this simply translates as inefficiency. They are hoping that their higher yields and lower costs will tempt the government eventually to open up the rest of the mining sector to them, and this debate is unlikely to go away in the near future. CODELCO's answer has been a slow process of modernization, and an attempt to add value to its resources by moving into refining the ore and producing pure copper cathodes, so that more of the industry's profits stay in the country.

Boom and Bust

This debate over the ownership of the copper industry raises troublesome ghosts from the past. Nowhere are these more present than in the deserted skeleton of a town like Humberstone, in the northern Atacama desert. Here, huge stone buildings and echoing mine-workings are a reminder of an earlier boom which brought immense wealth to the region, only to disappear almost overnight.

Humberstone and other towns in the Atacama were the center of the Chilean nitrate industry. After Chile had established its control over them in the 1880s War of the Pacific, it was mostly British-owned companies which exploited the mineral. By the end of the nineteenth century, the population in the north had doubled. Although a great proportion of the profits went abroad with the nitrates, the mines helped to form the modern Chilean state, which relied on revenues from this one export commodity to finance infrastructure and social projects for the whole population as Chile expanded at the turn of the century.

Nitrate production boomed in the years leading up to the First World War. During the war, however, German chemists invented a process for making artificial nitrates, which marked the beginning of the end for the industry. Nitrate production went into further decline during the Depression years, and although it flourished again briefly in the 1940s, it was no longer the large-scale vital industry it had once been. The towns gradually became deserted; Humberstone itself was finally closed in 1960 and is now a "heritage monument."

Nitrate ghost town

Julio Etchart/Reportage

Another area of mining which has met with an even more recent demise is coal production. This started far away from the nitrate fields, around the southern city of Concepción and the town of Lota, in the middle of the nineteenth century. Coal mining enjoyed its own boom because of the need for fuel for smelters in the north, and employed more than 6,000 miners. Industrial development in the middle of the twentieth century gave the coal industry a further boost, but the mines were still largely in private hands (the Cousiño family, who had started the first mine at Lota in 1852, were still one of the main proprietors) and gradually the coal became uneconomic to mine.

Nevertheless, as in Wales and other parts of the northern hemisphere, the mining activity around Lota created a tradition and a sense of community far beyond its economic importance. This meant that it was another highly emotional moment when the Allende government nationalized the coal mines in 1972, sparking great hopes of a worker-led revival of their fortunes. This did not happen, and lack of investment and the cheaper alternatives of hydroelectric power and gas saw the mines in a sharp decline throughout the 1980s. When the last mines at Lota were closed in 1997, there were protests by students and the thousand or more workers left, but there was no reprieve, and the mines closed after almost 150 years in operation. The government announced a $44 million development plan for the poor and backward Lota region.

John North, the "Nitrate King"

John Thomas North was a Yorkshire-born mechanic who emigrated to Valparaíso in 1866. He soon realized that there was more money to be made by trading and became a leading merchant in the booming port through which half of the country's imports passed. In the early 1880s North learnt of the Chilean government's decision to sell the nitrate factories captured from Peru to those who held the original bonds. He and a colleague bought up as many as possible of these bonds

John North

City Art Gallery, Leeds

in Lima, using capital borrowed from a British-owned bank in Valparaíso. This meant that at the end of the War of the Pacific, North was virtual owner of most of the valuable nitrate mines round Iquique and Tarapaca. He also bought up the water company and the railway. In London, where the price for nitrates was set, North operated virtual control in an early example of a cartel. For most of the 1880s, he ran a state within a state in northern Chile, earning himself the nickname "The Nitrate King." When President Balmaceda came to power and talked of nationalizing the railways and raising the tax on nitrate exports, North donated $150,000 to be used against him, so helping to finance the civil war of 1891. Although the rebels won that war, nitrate supply began to outstrip demand, and North found his poition increasingly threatened. Appropriately perhaps, he died of a seizure in London in 1896 while chairing a meeting of one of his companies, the Buena Ventura Nitrate Company.

Diversification

For some years in the 1970s, when revenues from copper accounted for 70 to 80 per cent of export earnings, it seemed that Chile could again fall into the same trap of over-dependence on a single commodity. Great efforts were therefore made throughout the 1980s to diversify into what were known as "non-traditional" exports, and this has reduced reliance on copper to a significant extent. Dependence on copper for export revenue fell from 75 per cent in 1970 to under 50 per cent a decade later, as a whole range of new commodities were developed.

Forestry

One of the most active sectors has been forestry. This was one of the first areas to be opened up to foreign companies by the Pinochet regime, which in 1974 passed legislation offering tax exemptions for firms clearing the native forest and replanting with pines and other industrial timber. Altogether, a fifth of Chile's landscape is forested, around 90 million acres in total. Of this, less than five million acres have been planted; with the recent expansion in the sector, this could rise to twelve million acres by the end of the century. Foreign companies which have invested in Chilean forestry have been encouraged by the fact that sunshine, high rainfall, and the cool Humboldt current offshore seem to create ideal climatic conditions for northwestern pines to grow. This has led to a rapid expansion around Puerto Aisén in the far south. Puerto Montt has also become an important port for wood-chips and logs, as new plantations of pine and eucalyptus come to maturity. Altogether, the forestry industry now includes over 700 companies and has a turnover of $1.5 billion each year. As with the mining sector, environmentalists warn that in this rush to expand, not enough attention is being paid to sustainability. They already speak of the exhaustion of the soils, of the changing nature of the landscape having harmful effects on diversity of wildlife and local biology, and the possible negative effects on tourism, also a major income earner in the south of Chile.

Not all rainforest is jungle. In the south of Chile, native beech, larches, and the monkey puzzle araucaria trees thrive in the wet weather and create a rainforest all of their own. Since the late 1970s, Chile's forests have quickly become merely another export commodity. This in turn has led to efforts by environmentalists and others to protect at least some of this precious first-growth forest, where 4,000-year-old trees are common. One such recent effort, by the U.S. businessman and ecologist Douglas Tomkins, has raised a huge controversy.

Tomkins, who first went to Chile in the 1970s as a member of the U.S. ski team, has been going back ever since. From the start of the 1990s, he has been buying up land in the far south between Río Negro and Chaitén. His intention, he says, is to create a 750,000-acre private nature park, to be called Pumalín. Having bought two main areas, Tomkins ran into opposition from the government which blocked his plan to buy a third, which would link the two others. Many Chileans have felt uneasy that such a large portion of Chilean territory should be owned by a foreigner, whatever he intends to do with it. Some right-wing politicians have even argued that because Tomkins' land extends from the ocean up to the Argentine border, Chile itself would be cut in two by a foreign power if the sale of the last piece were to be allowed. In mid-1997 the Chilean government agreed to the project on condition that the park be managed by a Chilean trust and a large proportion of it remain accessible to the public.

Tomkins himself responds by pointing out that the government sees no problem in selling the right to exploit huge tracts of forest to foreign logging and wood-chip companies, so why should his proposal, which would safeguard the original forest, be so controversial? He claims that the park would be run by a Chilean foundation: parts of it would be open to the public, others would be set aside for scientific research, while still others would be left completely untouched. The government, which lacks the funds to make the area a public national park, is faced with a dilemma that can only become more acute if the same economic model is followed in the future: how can it put a proper price on its natural resources, and avoid them being depleted? Recent studies commissioned from the French forestry agency into the effects of current logging policy on the native *lenga* wood, for example, conclude that the companies felling it for export treat forests like mines, to be stripped of their resources and then abandoned, so that within 30 years there is a danger of all the native lenga wood disappearing.

Fishing

Similar growth has been seen in Chile's fishing industry. Once again, this expansion has been based on allowing foreign firms, especially Japanese companies, to come in and trade. They have brought new methods which have produced spectacular results, but which have also raised fears about their longer-term sustainability. Salmon farming has been one of the most successful growth areas. In 1979, the industry was revolutionized by the introduction of floating cages in the southern lakes and coastal inlets. By the mid-1990s, these new techniques meant that Chile was second only to Norway in the export of farmed salmon, most of it destined for Japan. Thanks to the abundant fish stocks in the cold Humboldt current, in recent years there has also been spectacular growth in Chile's fishmeal industry, so that by 1995 it was the country's fourth largest export earner, after copper, paper pulp, and fresh fruit.

Fruit

Fresh fruit exports are another element in the considerable growth of Chile's agricultural sector, once again based on the exploitation of new products and modernization. During Spanish colonial times, the Central Valley of Chile was famous for its wheat and cattle. In the nineteenth century, it was Chilean crops which fed the western expansion of the USA during the California gold rush and the conquest of the West. But the construction of the Panama Canal, together with competition from other countries such as Australia, Canada, and Argentina, put paid to Chile's role as an agricultural exporter. Another obstacle was a pattern of landholding which created a few huge estates and thousands of tiny, unprofitable holdings, but not many middle-sized modern concerns, with the result that by the middle of the twentieth century, Chile was importing many of its basic foodstuffs.

Wine production   *Jason P Howe/South American Pictures*

After the attempts at land reform in the 1960s and early 1970s, the process was reversed under General Pinochet. About a third of the expropriated land was returned to its original owners. Another third stayed with the new owners, while much of the rest was sold off. This process brought in new owners with new ideas and fresh capital, which heralded a rapid expansion of the sector. The most dynamic area of development came with the production of soft fruit in the protected regions from Copiapó down through the Central Valley. By the mid-1990s, Chile had captured fifteen per cent of the world fruit export market, including over 40 per cent of the lucrative winter market for the northern hemisphere. While grapes and apples continued to be the most important exports, new developments included everything from blackberries to kiwi fruit.

The Wine Industry

The most spectacular advances in the agricultural sector, however, have been in Chile's wine industry. Although vines were brought hundreds of years ago by the Spaniards, and benefited from the fact that they were never attacked by the diseases such as phylloxera which wiped out many European vines in the nineteenth century, until the end of the 1970s, it was a small, non-industrialized business, often family-run. But by the mid-1990s, Chile was the third exporter of wines to the United States after France and Italy, outstripping even Spain. In the early 1980s, the value of wine exports was around $10 million; by 1994 this had risen to over $140 million. Both Spanish and French firms such as the Rothschild family have invested in Chilean vineyards in recent years, and are attempting to improve the quality of the wines, so that the industry seems destined to continue to grow.

Yet even the supposedly free-market world of the 1990s has its limits, as an unusual trade war recently showed. Pisco is Chile's national drink, made from fermented moscatel grapes grown mostly in the *norte chico*. Faced with an influx of Scotch whisky after the lowering of tariff barriers in the 1980s, the pisco producers successfully complained to the government, which raised the tariff to 70 per cent, while keeping pisco at 25 per cent. The Scottish distillers successfully appealed to the World Trade Organization on the grounds of unfair discrimination, but the Chilean government is still hesitating to comply, fearful of the reaction of local producers. In addition to this kind of problem, Chile has also found that it can sometimes be a victim of its own success. In 1993, the European Union closed the doors on Chilean apple exports, causing a crisis for the Central Valley producers. Worse still, when it was discovered that kiwi fruit could grow in almost every temperate country, there was a world-wide glut of the fruit which made it uneconomic to produce in Chile.

The Neo-Liberal Revolution

The huge changes in the Chilean economy are the legacy of attempts by General Pinochet and his advisers to radically alter the basic structures of the country. The main planks of this program were a reduction in state involvement in many areas, the opening of the Chilean market to products from other countries by tariff reductions, and the encouragement of private national and international investment to fuel growth. By 1980, Chile was one of the most free-market economies in the world, with the lowest tariff barriers (on average, ten per cent) anywhere. Liberal laws on taxation and the remittance of profits began to attract foreign investors, principally in the mining sector, who arrived in greater numbers from 1987 onwards when privatization accelerated.

In order to reduce state involvement in the economy, some 160 government-owned concerns were sold off between 1975 and 1989, together with sixteen banks and over 3,500 agricultural firms, mines, and property holdings. As the military regime was leaving power in the late 1980s, there was a second, more extensive, wave of sell-offs, which included many of the utility companies, the state airlines, and communications networks. This gave rise to the criticism that many of the privatized concerns simply ended up in the hands of companies controlled by members of the armed forces.

The argument behind the privatization process was that many of the state-sector enterprises were loss-making, and that their sale made it easier to balance the government budget. There was also a more general ideological aversion to the very notion of state ownership as an obstacle to free-market development. Critics in the unions and the left-wing parties, meanwhile, accused the government of selling many of the state-owned companies too cheaply and of not establishing proper controls for prices and consumer satisfaction in sectors like the utility companies after their privatization. One notorious example is that of the sugar-refining company, IANSA, sold off in 1985 for $34 million, even though its estimated value was put at around $80 million. In the first three years after privatization, company profits were $52 million, far higher than the price paid for the entire company.

In addition to the privatization drive, Chilean industry became more competitive because of strict controls imposed on labor. Trade unionists were one of the main groups targeted in the repression after the 1973 coup, and when the military government brought in a new Labor Code in 1979, this severely limited the rights of workers to organize. The Code only permitted workers employed continuously for more than six months (often not the case in the agricultural sector, for example) to join a union. It allowed companies to dismiss workers en masse "for business needs," and greatly restricted the conditions under which strikes were deemed legal. While the right to strike still nominally exists, companies can dismiss strikers after 30 days and employ new staff in their place. Since the return of civilian rule, the trade union movement, which is largely dominated by the Christian Democrats, has preferred compromise to confrontation, arguing that the continued growth of the economy is the most important guarantee of workers' benefits.

Economic Growth and the "Miracle"

Growth has by no means been steady since Pinochet and the "Chicago Boys" began to restructure the Chilean economy. A damaging recession took place in 1975 soon after the military government seized power. After several years of expansion in the late 1970s, the economy went into another severe recession in 1981, as copper prices reached their lowest point since the Second World War. Many companies went bankrupt, a full-scale crisis erupted among the recently deregulated banks, and the economy shrank by a startling 14.1 per cent in 1982. Imports declined by a half, while Chile's external debt rose to more than $17 billion, requiring 80 per cent of export earnings for debt-servicing.

Under the aegis of the International Monetary Fund (IMF), the government devalued the peso by 45 per cent in 1982 in a bid to stop the tide of imports and make exports more competitive. A more pragmatic economic policy also replaced the extreme monetarism of the Chicago Boys, with the emphasis on sustainable growth through diversified exports. From 1985, growth began to recover, averaging an annual 5.5 per cent for the rest of the decade. At a time when other Latin American countries

Santiago's business district   *Julio Etchart/Reportage*

were experiencing stubborn recessions, Chile stood out as the region's "miracle," achieving a growth rate of ten per cent in 1989 alone.

The return of civilian rule brought a continuation of the growth pattern, and during the four years of the Aylwin government Chile's GDP grew on average by 6.2 per cent a year, the best record of any Chilean government. Per capita GDP in 1993 was twenty per cent higher than at the end of 1989, as Chile's economy expanded three times faster than the rest of Latin America. Recent economic performance has also been impressive, with growth rates of 8.5 per cent in 1997 and 7.2 per cent in 1996.

In many ways, Chile has been an economic success story. With a wide and diversified range of exports, assisted by its unusually varied climate and mineral deposits, the country has been able to steadily improve its balance of payments and win large slices of competitive foreign markets. Unemployment has tumbled from heights of around twenty per cent in the early 1980s to about five per cent currently. Inflation has been brought down from three figures in the 1970s to a manageable annual average of five or six per cent, and the government has consistently run a fiscal surplus.

Yet the questions remain: is the "miracle" sustainable, and what has been its social cost? Critics point out that Chile remains largely an exporter of primary commodities rather than manufactured goods, and that these are always vulnerable to volatile world markets. Overproduction and foreign competition, as in the case of kiwi fruit, are real threats to any agricultural export, while intensive agri-business production inevitably results in environmental degradation caused by the over-use of pesticides and other inputs. The government's neo-liberal stance means that it is unwilling to intervene too directly in the economy by encouraging manufacturing with incentives and protection. As a result, Chile's economy, in the medium term at least, is likely to remain over-dependent on unpredictable commodities.

The radical economic cahnges of the neo-liberal model have taken a heavy toll on Chileans themselves. "Flexible" working practices have replaced secure jobs, creating insecurity at work and at home. Although most people are now less poor than twenty years ago, thanks to overall growth, inequalities have sharpened rather than declined. The mantras of privatization and the free market have been more enthusiastically embraced by a minority of entrepreneurs than by the majority of middle- and working-class families.

Chile's New Generation

The way that the social aspects of recent economic policy have drastically altered Chile can be seen in the lives of people like Carlos Valenzuela. Carlos is a Santiago thirty-something. He has a managerial job in one of the newly privatized big companies. He has a wife and two children, with whom he lives in a recently-built apartment up in a suburb in the hills which ring the capital. He drives a foreign car and has been to Europe on vacation for the first time recently, in addition to his usual vacation down on the coast.

But it is the way in which he pays for his health care and his pension that makes him so different from his parents' generation. Carlos pays a monthly health care contribution to a health insurance company which covers him for whatever care he needs. His wife does the same, and their two children are also covered. Carlos cannot understand why his father and mother still insist on subsidizing the national health service: since 1981, they have had the choice to opt out, but for some reason prefer to stay with the system they have known all their lives. Even his mother has noticed, however, that the doctors in the national medical service seem mostly very young and inexperienced, and that the hospital in the small provincial town where they live does not seem to have much modern equipment.

Carlos was also part of the first generation to start paying for pensions through a private pension fund. These funds were also launched when he started work, early in the 1980s. He has been paying into it for almost twenty years now, but cannot really explain to his father what he is going to get out of it when he eventually retires. His father still has the state pension from the old system, but Carlos knows that by the time he is of retiring age in 2020 that system will not exist any more. These pension funds, the *administradoras de fondos de pensiones* or AFPs, have grown enormously since the early 1980s, largely because they have been taking money in from relatively young people like Carlos, and have not yet had to pay out much in actual pensions. Accordingly, they have been seen as one of the great success stories of Chile's economic "miracle." The money invested by the pension funds in the Chilean economy accounts for over 40 per cent of GDP, helping the level of national savings in Chile to be over 25 per cent, far higher than in any neighboring countries and reducing the need for fickle foreign investment.

But not everyone is in the same fortunate, well-planned position as Carlos. Those who have no steady job cannot get into the pension schemes, and in 1996, more than half of those who were officially registered were behind with payments. That same year the funds also experienced a sharp downturn in growth. Carlos's father also points out skeptically that the armed forces themselves do not contribute to the scheme, even though the idea was launched while they were in power. He sees the AFPs as a creation of this economic model, which could end up paying out far less than his son expects, especially if there is an economic crisis. His son says that he should have the choice of where and how to invest for his future; his father says the pension system is building inequality into society from the cradle to the grave.

But neither the military regime nor the two civilian governments which have followed have paid much attention to people like Carlos's father. The Christian Democrats claimed that their governments would stress "growth with equity." They have, however, relied heavily on continued growth to pull people out of poverty without intervening to any great extent to redistribute wealth. While there has been little redistribution of the national income, levels of earnings have risen in general.

Both Aylwin and Frei have shown themselves to be fully committed to the export-led economy that has brought such good results so far, choosing to ignore those critics who warn of exhaustion of the environment or potential problems of over-production. At the same time, they have done far less to stimulate national industry, apparently conceding that Chile is too small a market to allow firms any advantage of scale. As a result, Chile remains primarily an exporter of mineral and agricultural commodities, with relatively little value added to exports through manufacturing.

There has also been little emphasis on developing human potential, a feature of the so-called "Asian Tiger" economies, with which Chile has been compared. As one author has pointed out:

> Successful developing countries get into computers, not kiwi fruit, yet the Chilean government shows a massive indifference to the country's technological base. While the business courses are packed, in 1992 only three students graduated in math and four in physics from the University of Chile.

Although the country is widely seen as a paragon of neo-liberal values and state non-intervention, it remains the case that Chile's chief export earner, copper, is still in state hands. There are increasing pressures for this industry to be privatized as well and to get the Chuquicamata trucks working not just 17 hours a day, but 23, as they would in some competitor countries. Chile's continued economic success seems to lie in future governments using their position to make the slogan of "growth with equity" into a reality, so that it is not simply macro-economic statistics which improve, but the quality of life for a majority of Chileans.

New Markets

In order to guarantee continuing success for this economic model, Chile now has to look for fresh markets for its exports. It is attempting to follow the USA, Canada, and Mexico in becoming the next member of the North American Free Trade Agreement (NAFTA), which should further boost agricultural sales in the U.S. and Canadian markets. To this end, President Clinton promised President Frei in 1997 that he would seek "fast track" congressional approval for Chile to join NAFTA at the earliest possible date. Chile has also recently become an associate member of Mercosur, the free-trade agreement between Argentina, Brazil, Paraguay, and Uruguay. Here, Chile's role would be rather different in that it would hope to use its years of experience in the financial and banking sector to be a supplier of services and expertise as the other countries follow the same export-led path that it adopted several years before any of them. Chile now hopes that free-trade policies will give it a dominant rather than a dependent position in its international trading relationships.

4   SOCIETY: CONSUMING PASSIONS

The Italian film star Sophia Loren visited Santiago not long ago. She did not come to make a film or even to see friends, but to open a huge new shopping mall in Las Condes, a smart suburb of the capital. Over the past twenty years, above all in Santiago and the rich resort towns of the coast, conspicuous consumption has replaced the sense of sobriety which traditionally earned Chileans the nickname of the "English of Latin America."

This consumerism is a direct result of the radical economic policies first introduced by the Pinochet regime. With import tariffs lowered, Chileans for the first time could buy French perfumes, Japanese cars and electrical goods, and Scotch whisky. Between 1976 and 1981, more than two million TV sets are said to have been imported into Chile. Figures also show that in 1980, all the color TV sets and 98 per cent of the foreign cars were bought by the wealthiest fifth of the population, while the poorest twenty per cent bought almost no imported goods at all. This gap between the buying power of the rich and the poor has gone on increasing even under the civilian governments of the 1990s.

At times, this "shop-til-you-drop" craze seems almost like a psychosis: one Chilean comedian gives three examples of the way in which it affects behavior. He says that many Chileans will go to the new hyper-markets stocked with all kinds of foreign goods, get a trolley and walk round the aisles filling it. They naturally meet all their neighbors in the store, chat and compare purchases. But when they are approaching the checkout, they park their trolley in a corner, and leave as quickly as they can with only a couple of items, because they cannot afford anything more. He also says that the *carabineros* or traffic police who stop motorists for illegally using mobile phones in their cars discover that 60 per cent of them are in fact toys or wooden imitations. He also jokes at the way in which many of those same drivers will speed along in the hot summer months with all their car windows tight shut, to give the impression that they have air-conditioning.

Crisis of Trust

More seriously, this equation of personal value with conspicuous consumption has eaten away at more traditional notions of solidarity and community which had been deeply rooted in Chile. In part, this is due to the change from a peasant, country-based society to a predominantly urban

A shopping mall in
central Santiago

*Julio Etchart/
Reportage*

one. It is also a symptom of the fact that the younger generation now travels more both within Chile and abroad, and has looser ties to the family. But, more significantly, it is undeniably a consequence of both the political and economic atmosphere of the last twenty years.

Another noticeable aspect of this sweeping change is the depoliticization of Chilean society. In the past, and well before the turbulent years of Allende's Popular Unity government and the 1973 coup, Chileans loved to discuss political ideas and affiliations in the way other nations discuss the weather or food. Nowadays, there seems to be almost no interest in politics. The 1994 presidential elections, the first to offer choice between political parties for over twenty years, evoked only lukewarm interest, particularly among young people who were voting for the first time. This is partly a legacy of the repression of the 1970s and 1980s, when it could be very dangerous to express political opinions. But there is also a widespread feeling that today's party politicians are a remote and self-serving elite, distant from the real problems of the populace, who manage to come out on top whatever happens. This has created a considerable sense of cynicism and apathy. One Chilean commentator quotes the example of a former Marxist politician who was prominent in Allende's government, but is now running one of the privatized utility firms.

Suspicion of other people's conduct and motives extends beyond politicians and has affected personal relations in general. The experience of the coup and the tortures and murders which followed it has had a profound impact throughout Chile. In addition to the deaths and disappearances, more than 40,000 Chileans were arrested at some point during the Pinochet years for suspected subversive activities; many more lost their jobs or saw their careers blighted. This meant that almost every family in the country was affected in some way by the repression. The result has been a crisis of trust which Ricardo Lagos, the Socialist Party leader described to the Argentine journalist Jácobo Timerman as:

> The drama of a country that has seen emerge from its own entrails those who murder, torture, cut throats, and now even burn other human beings, and who brazenly walk the streets at our side, without our

understanding where these people came from, or how it was possible that our society give origin to this, to these thousands who seem to be normal beings. This is an element of moral crisis in a society, which must be treated with the seriousness it requires, not only by dealing with those who must be brought to justice, but, beyond that, by determining how a society could come to this.

This kind of questioning has come most insistently from the several hundred thousand Chileans who left the country after the coup, either because of direct persecution or because they found it impossible to stay. Their experience on returning has been very mixed; many have reintegrated successfully into society, while others have been among those most responsible for hastening the change to a more individualistic, consumer society. A large number, too, have found it impossible to resettle and have chosen to go and live abroad again. In conversation, those who have opted to leave Chile a second time speak of their feeling that Chilean society as a whole has not learnt from the experiences of the past twenty years, but has preferred to bury everything in silence, almost as if it never happened.

The Military

Part of the distrust which many Chileans feel towards the professional politicians arises from the way in which they have compromised with the armed forces, even after the military's withdrawal from government in 1989. Spending on the armed forces in 1994 was 3.5 per cent of GDP, the highest proportion in all Latin America. General Pinochet continues as commander-in-chief of the army until 1998, when, aged 81 and after 63 years in the army, he intends to become a senator for life. He has used his position to block any attempts to find ways around the amnesty for human rights abuses which the military government passed in 1978. One example of this kind of conflict came in 1995 when there was a prolonged stand-off over the arrest of the former head of the secret police, General Contreras. The general had been condemned to seven years' jail for his part in the killing of Orlando Letelier, a minister in the Allende's government who was blown up in Washington, D.C. in what became an international scandal. General Pinochet and his army colleagues refused to hand Contreras over for several weeks, and threatened to come out onto the streets, until finally they grudgingly accepted the authority of the civilian court.

The civilian governments have had to accept the continuing legacy of the seventeen-year dictatorship in many other ways. There are still eight senators in parliament who were nominated by the military government rather than elected. So far this number has been sufficient to enable the right wing in Congress to block any moves to change the constitution.

Until the mid-1990s, local mayors were also appointed rather than elected. Despite all this, President Aylwin commented on leaving office that he considered General Pinochet to have been a guarantee of stability against anti-democratic elements in society, and declared that he had changed his opinion of him over his four years in office.

The attitude of the armed forces themselves towards the role they have played in society was summed up by General Pinochet himself. When asked in the mid-1990s if he felt there was any need to apologize for what the military had done, he retorted: "They're the ones who need to ask forgiveness for all the chaos and disorder they caused before September 11 [the date of the 1973 coup]. Who are we supposed to ask forgiveness from? From those who tried to kill me? From those who tried to destroy our fatherland? From whom?" There is little doubt that this is the feeling of most of the armed forces in Chile today. They have kept their powerful position as a society within a society. They consider that they successfully rescued the country from subversion in the early 1970s, that they forced the Argentines to back off in border disputes and choose to take over the Falklands/Malvinas Islands instead, mistakenly considering it an easier option. They still see themselves as the guarantors rather than the violators of democracy, and as such their subordination to constitutional rule is as yet far from complete.

The Churches

As in the rest of Latin America, the Catholic Church arrived in Chile with the Spanish colonizers and played an integral role in the conquest and settlement of the new territory. The 1925 constitution formally separated state and church, but the Catholic faith was so deep-rooted that it continued to enjoy great influence throughout society, particularly in education. This, together with the fact that there was no large scale immigration of people from other faiths (Jewish or Protestant) makes Chile a far more traditionally Catholic country than the other Southern Cone countries of Argentina or Uruguay.

The reforms in the Catholic Church ushered in by the second Vatican Council in 1962 were clearly reflected in Chile. On the one hand, part of the Church saw its work as being to help the poor, and became actively involved in the social reforms of the Frei and Allende governments. On the other, much of the hierarchy continued to insist that the Church should be entirely concerned with spiritual matters, and should shun any "political" role.

This tension came to a head after the 1973 coup. Priests who were working in the shanty towns, many of them foreign, were either expelled

Demonstration by relatives
of the disappeared

Julio Etchart/Reportage

from Chile or were persecuted. General Pinochet, a devout Catholic, expected the Church to support his actions, which in his view had been carried out in defense of "Western, Christian values." Most of the bishops did share his point of view, but the archbishop of Santiago, Cardinal Raúl Silva Hernández, was far more robust in his insistence on defending human rights. He helped to set up a Peace Committee to provide legal aid for victims of the repression, and when that was closed down by the military government in 1975, was personally responsible for founding the Vicariate of Solidarity. For long periods during the seventeen years of military rule, the Vicariate's ramshackle building, full of untidy offices and overworked volunteers, was the only place that the victims of persecution and their families could go for help. Other priests continued to work in the shanty towns, and some, such as the French missionary André Jarlan who was shot in 1984, paid with their lives.

Since the death of Cardinal Silva, and the return of civilian rule, the Catholic Church has reverted to a far more traditional role. It has continued to oppose the introduction of divorce or the right to abortion in Chile. In 1997, Catholic-owned television stations refused to carry a government campaign warning of the dangers of AIDS. In general, the Catholic Church has become much more conservative and defensive; as one Jesuit priest has remarked, "The young are conservative and the old are progressive." Those who attend Mass are more likely to be from the wealthy suburbs than from the shanty towns or even from among the professional middle classes.

The defensive attitude of the Catholic Church is in part a response to the inroads that other churches, notably the evangelical Protestants, are making in Chile. As in other countries of Latin America, the evangelical churches began to grow during the years of military repression, and since then their message of personal responsibility and direct spirituality has chimed in with the economic message of neo-liberalism. The new evangelicals are the would-be entrepreneurs from the lower middle classes, identifiable in Chile as everywhere else on the continent from Texas to Tierra del Fuego by their smart clean shirts, ball-point pens in blazer pockets, and plastic briefcases. By the mid-1990s, it was reported that as many as twenty per cent of Chileans were members of these new churches, with the Mormons, for example, claiming over 300,000 followers.

Colonia Dignidad

There have been German settlers in the south of Chile since the middle of the nineteenth century. Attracted by the region's lakes and mountains, they have generally been seen as industrious, respectable, and cooperative. But one German settlement, Colonia Dignidad, in the foothills of the Andes near the town of Parral, has an altogether more sinister reputation.

The colony was set up in 1961 by a German Baptist pastor called Paul Schaeffer. He came with his followers from the south of Germany to establish a Christian community which would have as little as possible to do with the outside world. Radios, televisions, and newspapers were banned from the colony, which supported itself from farming, brick-making, and other simple industries. The community prospered, and won over local people by offering work, the services of its medical clinic, and organizing schools and recreation for poor children.

It was after the 1973 military coup that Colonia Dignidad's reputation changed. A number of people who later went into exile were convinced that the installations there had been used as a torture center, with the full knowledge of the members. Other stories began to emerge of young people who had escaped from the colony, claiming that they had been physically and sexually maltreated.

Thanks to the protection of the authorities, no thorough investigation of the colony was ever carried out. When President Aylwin came to power, he withdrew the colony's tax-free status, but took no further measures against it. In November 1996, however, several more young people came forward and said that they were willing to testify against Schaeffer, by now in his seventies. In 1997, the police moved into Colonia Dignidad to take Paul Schaeffer in for questioning, but were unable to find him.

Rich and Poor

Sophia Loren came to open a mall owned by another Italian, Anacleto Angelini. He emigrated to Chile after the end of the Second World War, and is now Chile's richest individual, with a net fortune estimated at $2.3 billion. The way in which his company or *grupo económico* emerged greatly strengthened from the years of economic reform is typical of how wealth was increasingly concentrated in a few hands during the years of military rule. In the decade from 1978-1988, for example, the income of the wealthiest ten per cent in Chile grew by 83 per cent; according to a recent World Bank report, income inequalities in Chile are second only to Brazil in South America.

The Angelini Group started out in fishing in the northern ports. They then bought into a timber company in the south, and grew steadily through the 1960s and 1970s. In 1986, the Group benefited from the second round of the military government's sell-offs of public-sector industries by acquiring COPEC, the state oil company. Experts claim that this was sold at half its book price, and that the original investment is now worth almost twenty times the original outlay. In addition to expanding in the industrial sector, the Angelini Group have also moved into the main growth area in the economy, the service sector, and are now owners of Chile's largest insurance company, Cruz del Sur, as well as one of its largest pension fund administration firms. The complete list of the company's holdings includes coal mines, an electric company, hydroelectric plants, oil and natural gas production and distribution firms, a chain of home appliance stores, farms, real estate, saw mills, pulp mills, and the privatized port facilities from which all these timber products are exported. In all, the Angelini Group produces no less than five per cent of the country's exports.

Another example of how wealth has become increasingly concentrated is the Matte family group. Responsibility for this traditional forestry and paper concern was assumed in the early 1980s by Eliodoro Matte Larrain, who, naturally enough, had studied business at the University of Chicago in the 1970s. In 1982, the bank controlled by the Matte group was the only one not needing rescue by the Central Bank during the national financial crisis. Instead, it responded to the crisis by cutting its workforce from 5,000 to 3,500. When business started to pick up again, Matte quickly broadened the bank's base in the services and financial sector, so that today its assets represent almost seven per cent of Chile's GDP. Eliodoro explained the difference between his and his father's generation in the following terms: "We were different from our elders, totally committed to the notion of free enterprise ... It is crucial to retain liberal ideas, and we must be aggressive in defending them."

At the same time, these liberal ideas saw the percentage of national income derived from wages falling from 42.7 per cent in 1970, to less than 34 per cent in 1993. This period also witnessed sharply increased levels of poverty, which, according to government statistics, put some 45 per cent of Chileans below an acceptable income level by 1986. To the traditionally deprived groups of the rural poor, particularly among the indigenous populations in the north and in the south, and peasants with little or no land to work, were added huge numbers of workers who could only find seasonal harvesting jobs in the new fruit export industry, but had little or no prospect of working for the other nine months of the year. There was also the phenomenon of "white-collar poverty," involving thousands of state employees, teachers, or clerical workers laid off in the reorganization of the economy which took place during the late 1970s and 1980s.

Yet, despite growing inequalities, the military government did make some efforts to target those most in need. One of the "modernizations" it carried out was to transfer responsibility for housing and benefits to the local level. In some cases, mayors and officials set up work schemes or communal kitchens to help the most needy, although there was often great resentment at this kind of forced aid.

General Pinochet also placed great emphasis on trying to reduce Chile's huge housing deficit, partly to avoid any more *tomas* or takeovers of land by people desperate for somewhere to live, which had been a feature of the Allende years. In this way, some 420,000 state-subsidized housing units were built during his regime. This still left a far larger number of Chileans still seeking a decent place to live; a survey in 1983 found that more than 800,000 people in the large towns and cities were sleeping four or more to one bedroom.

The civilian governments which followed military rule have placed all their hopes on economic growth alleviating poverty. There has been little direct redistribution of the national income, although spending on health, housing, and benefits has increased. According to government statistics in 1997, there were still some 800,000 Chileans living in absolute poverty, with an income of less than around $30 a month. As one journalist has put it: "There are two Chiles, one with credit cards and computers, and one that is just trying to survive."

Women

Although Chilean women won the vote in 1949, they are still very much underrepresented on the national political scene, even if they are prominent in politics at a local level and in many of the professions. Although women were at the forefront of the political struggles of the early 1970s, they became even more involved under the military government. With political parties and trade unions, both traditionally male-dominated, banned, a new generation of grassroots social movements, such as shanty town organizations and soup kitchens, filled the political vacuum. Many of these were headed by women. *democracia en el país y en la casa* ("Democracy in the country and in the home") was one of the most common rallying cries of this movement, which did have some success in changing ingrained male attitudes. However, many women's organizations have found it hard to cope with the return to democracy, during which power has largely reverted to male-run political parties.

Figures from 1987 showed that women's average earnings were only 71 per cent of those of men, and little progress has been made since. It also appears that it is middle-class, educated women who have made most eco-

An *arpillera* showing a raid on a shanty town   *CAFOD*

nomic and social advances in the past generation. Poorer women still have larger families, are far more likely to be single parents, and to believe with 23-year-old Nora that: "I want to have a baby so that I can have something of my own, because I've never had anything of my own."

Political Patchworks

In the 1970s and 1980s they appeared on living room walls from Berlin to Vancouver. Small patchworks with doll-like figures and a slogan referring to the harsh realities of life in Chile under the dictatorship: "No to torture!" "Where are our loved ones?" "Bread, Freedom, Justice." These were the *arpilleras,* embroidered brightly-colored cloth pictures which spoke movingly and directly to many people who knew little of Chile. They were produced by groups of women from the poorer areas of Santiago and other towns, who had first met each other while searching for news of loved ones arrested or abducted by the security forces. They were organized into workshops by the Catholic Vicariate of Solidarity or other groups, and became the focus for other communal activities such as soup kitchens and human rights work. In the 1970s and 1980s, hundreds of women were engaged in making these patchworks which, in their combination of a direct political message and genuine artistic creation, were unique. But in 1991, the Vicariate decided to close down its workshops. Sales to other countries dwindled, and gradually the numbers of women still making the *arpilleras* fell to around a dozen. Visiting these women in 1994, the Chilean exile writer Marjorie Agosín concluded, "The precarious, almost abandoned situation of the *arpilleristas* coincides with the state of absolute silence with respect to human rights in Chile today."

Education and young people

When appointed rector of the University of Chile, the general could think of no better way of impressing his new colleagues and students than to parachute into the grounds of the university. This was the perfect symbol of the Pinochet approach to the universities, which were all put under

Women sewing *arpilleras*   *Julio Etchart/Reportage*

military command, while staff and students were weeded out for "subversive activities." Between 1973 and 1975, around 20,000 of them were forced to leave. Teaching returned to traditional syllabuses and methods, often under the watchful eye of members of the security forces. Student organizations were broken up, grants reduced, and enrollments cut back.

Alongside repression and censorship, the new economic policies were applied in the educational sector as elsewhere. The traditional state institutions like the University of Chile, which runs everything from a TV station to a ballet company and one of the country's best soccer teams, were challenged by new, private colleges. These new institutions took only paying students; their courses were market-oriented, in business, legal, or financial subjects; government supervision was minimal. When the rector of one such college was challenged that the private academies had no resources and could offer little more than a blackboard and chalk, he retorted: "I'm sure Einstein used chalk and a blackboard when he was demonstrating the Theory of Relativity. The importance is not so much the facilities, but the quality of the teaching." Thanks to this gung-ho spirit, there were more than 30 of these new universities by the mid-1990s, catering to more than 20,000 students.

Including those attending other new technical universities, the number of students in higher education has now more than doubled to over 250,000, while the higher education budget has been halved. Quite what these students will do after they graduate is another matter (in 1995, for example, there were 800 students graduating in journalism studies, when there are only an estimated 3,000 paid journalists in the whole country). "Well, we'll have the world's best educated bus and taxi drivers," one university lecturer commented, only half-jokingly.

This struggle to find a job is just one of the many challenges facing the 40 per cent of Chileans who are under 21. Although the education system guarantees literacy and basic skills, schools are often where inequality starts. Half of Chile's three million schoolchildren attend private schools, many of them religious. A generation of schooling under a repressive military regime, for many years also with a nighttime curfew which restricted social activities, has led to young people who, according to a 1987 survey, almost never discuss politics or democracy. This conclusion was confirmed by the 1994 elections, when few young people took any active part in the campaigning. It was the Green candidate Manfred Max-Neef who aroused most enthusiasm among first-time voters, who in general appear distrustful of the experiences of the older generations, but are unable to articulate a clear response of their own to the consumerist society in which they find themselves.

Alien Nation

The proliferation of "alienating consumerism" was one of the main criticisms leveled against the model of society being created by General Pinochet and his economic team by labor leaders in a special supplement of the left-wing magazine *Análisis* in 1983. They also condemned "individualism, profit, and unchecked competition" as destroying the values of solidarity and community which the trade union movement stood for. Ironically, *Análisis*, a vital source of debate and information in the military years, has since closed down for lack of subscribers, and the unions are weakened and can no longer claim to speak for the majority of Chileans.

A more recent survey, published in the newspaper *La Epoca* in 1996, shows the contemporary pressures put on individuals who try to conform to the new economic and social model. According to the World Health Organization, Chile has the third highest level of child abuse in the world and the second highest level of gastric cancer, after Japan. The WHO has also discovered that around a half of all visits to the state health system are the result of psychological problems such as depression or anxiety. Other statistics testify to the stress associated with the "Chilean miracle." Suicides trebled between 1970 and 1991. A commission on health reporting to the country's Chamber of Deputies has recently found that Chile has the highest rate of alcohol consumption in Latin America, and the highest rate of consumption of amphetamines.

5   CULTURE: LAND OF POETS

"Turn over any stone in Chile," Pablo Neruda once said, "and you'll find a poet." Whether he meant it kindly or not, it is certainly true that poetry seems an almost natural phenomenon in Chile, and has been for centuries. *La Araucana*, the first epic of the Americas, was written by Alonso de Ercilla, one of the Spanish soldiers who came to conquer Chile in the sixteenth century. After years of fighting the indigenous Mapuche in the south, he wrote his lengthy poem, remarkable for the appreciation it shows of the people he had been fighting only a few years before:

> We it was who set out to destroy
> all we came upon in our path
> forcing a way with our usual arrogance
> and opening the door to all these ills;
> as their ancient laws became corrupted
> ruined by a stream of insults
> and soon greed planted its banner
> more firmly than ever before.

Since then, attitudes to Chile's indigenous peoples and their culture have rarely been so enlightened. They are occasionally evoked and romanticized as part of the country's folklore, but only recently has there been any real appreciation or understanding of the kinds of animist beliefs around which the Aymara and Mapuche base their lives. The two groups are mostly known for the handicrafts they produce, which vary from the weaving of colorful ponchos and braids to silver jewelry and pottery.

Neruda and Poetry

In this century, Chile has produced two poets whose stature has won them international fame and the Nobel prize for literature. The first was Gabriela Mistral, who was also the first Latin American to win the distinction. A schoolteacher from the northern valley of the Elqui, her verses are Romantic and passionate, colored by her unrequited love for a man who committed suicide while still very young. Though much of her work was written early in the century, she was awarded the Nobel prize in 1945, and died in 1957.

At one point, Gabriela Mistral was the head teacher of a school where the young Neftalí Reyes studied. Neftalí, who later took the pseudonym Pablo Neruda, was to become by far the most influential poet not only in Chile, but in the whole of Latin America. From his early works such as

Young Chileans at
Neruda's grave

Hugh O'Shaughnessy

Residence on Earth (1935), to his encyclopedic *Canto General* (1950), or his *Elemental Odes* (1961), he showed an appetite for making poetry out of everything in life and a mastery of the means of expression he chose which makes him the poetic equivalent of someone like Pablo Picasso. Like Picasso too, he became something of a prisoner of his own fame, and his political beliefs as a staunch communist led him at times to write such oddities as an ode in praise of Stalin. Others have criticized his attitude towards women, and see some of his love poetry as also being too facile. Yet the fact remains, as the Argentine writer Jácobo Timerman has put it: "His words and his rhythms will forever be the only expression that we Latin Americans have when our heart overflows with love for another human or with love of the universe." And anyone who writes an "Ode to a Pair of Socks" cannot be all bad.

Neruda has been such a towering figure in Chilean poetry that most other poets have struggled to find a distinctive voice of their own. One who has achieved it by deliberately writing what he calls "anti-poetry" is Nicanor Parra. His caustic humor, together with his determination to deflate all kinds of rhetoric, have given him a large following in Chile. In the 1990s it is his voice which appears to attract the new generation of poets, who have assimilated the experiences of the Pinochet years and are experimenting with language in a way that avoids direct political expression.

Chileanisms

Chilean Spanish is full of expressions peculiar to the country, some of them very idiosyncratic:

Un Barros Luco: a sandwich of meat and cheese, named after the president whose favorite snack this was.

Mas perdido que el Teniente Bello: literally, more lost than Lieutenant Bello, or completely lost, after a Chilean pilot who disappeared in the Andes on a flight of only 60 miles.

Capitán Araya embarca a todos y se queda en la playa: Captain Araya sends the others off and stays on the beach — someone who leads from the rear, sending others off to do the dirty work but keeping his own hands clean.

Caracol: a snail, but also a name for the new shopping malls, the first of which were built in a circular form like a snail, with walkways winding back on themselves.

Gallo: common expression for guy; *ten cuidado con estos gallos, son super pillos:* "watch out for those guys, they're really sharp."

Guagua: baby. Not to be confused with a Cuban guagua, a bus.

Huevón: All-purpose word to express exasperation at someone, either with affection or without. Nearest equivalent is "asshole," although this refers to a different part of the anatomy.

La huifa!: expression of joy, surprise, etc. One of very few indigenous expressions to have been incorporated into Chilean Spanish.

Lookear: to go window shopping in one of the new shopping malls.

Pacos: police.

Paquete chileno: a con trick involving bundle of fake notes and personal greed.

Penca: boring, dull.

Ya po!: That's enough!

Often the best Chilean poetry has been close to music. One of the best-known examples of this combination was another member of the Parra family, Nicanor's sister, Violeta. It was she who brought new life to Chilean folk music in the 1960s, helping to start what became known as *la nueva canción chilena* (New Chilean Song). Her *décimas* and simple songs about life and love (the most famous being *Gracias a la vida* or "Thanks to Life") were avidly taken up not just by young, socially committed Chileans but by audiences throughout Latin America. In the late 1960s, her words brought a new social dimension to songs:

> And his conscience said at last:
> sing of man in his sorrow,
> in his poverty, in his sweat,
> in his reason for being alive.

Commitment and Exile

Violeta Parra also revived the tradition of *peñas,* or folk song evenings, with guitars and *charangos,* the small Andean stringed instruments. Her poignant voice and her chaotic, tragic life (she committed suicide in 1967) reinvented the romantic troubadour tradition for a whole generation. She was often joined by her children Isabel and Angel and the guitarist Victor Jara. Jara became a tragic symbol of how this whole enthusiastic, romantic, socially committed artistic spirit was destroyed when, after the September 1973 military coup, he was captured and taken with thousands of other

Ariel Dorfman   *Julio Etchart/Reportage*

prisoners to the National Stadium in Santiago to be tortured and killed. Many other popular musicians and poets fled abroad after the coup, and thanks to groups such as Quilapayún or Inti-Illimani, this kind of committed Chilean music became known in many other countries.

Something similar occurred in the field of literature, as it was writers who left Chile in the 1970s who became best known internationally, often leading to friction with those who had stayed and tried to make their contribution throughout the Pinochet years. Isabel Allende, whose *House of the Spirits* (1985), the most widely-read Latin American novel after García Márquez's *A Hundred Years of Solitude*, is one such example. She was harshly criticized in Chile for simply using the country as a backdrop for her magical creations, as well as for exploiting the fact that she was President Allende's niece.

Similar controversy has surrounded Ariel Dorfman. He became popular in university circles in Chile during the early 1970s for books like *How to Read Donald Duck*, an intelligent and timely essay on how U.S. cultural imperialism can appear in any number of disguises, including the most absurd. After the military takeover, Dorfman went to live abroad, and again angered some other Chilean writers and critics by using themes such as torture and repression in works such as *Widows,* or *Death and the Maiden*, which became an internationally successful play and then a film, in a way which they felt was exploiting suffering. It was also true, of course, that these works played key roles in educating U.S. and European audiences about Chilean realities and history.

Another exile was Antonio Skármeta, whose novel *Burning Patience,* about the relation between an illiterate postman and Pablo Neruda, his only customer on Isla Negra, became the successful film *Il Postino* (The Postman). The resentment felt against successful writers such as Skármeta is more than mere literary jealousy. In many ways, it seems as though literary and artistic circles in Chile were those which felt most betrayed by their colleagues who left the country. Those who stayed tried often to reflect the violence and repression imposed on an entire society in their work, either in the performance work of people like Raúl Zurita and Damiela Eltit, or the photography and video works of artists such as Roser Bru.

Among the divisions caused by Chile's recent political history, it was perhaps a novelist from an older generation who best came to grips with what was happening to the country under Pinochet. José Donoso had become well-known internationally in the 1970s as part of the so-called "boom" of Latin American fiction with his novel *The Obscene Bird of Night* (1973). His later books such as *A House in the Country* (1983), *Curfew* (1988), or the four short novels *Cuatro para Delfina* explore the *nouveaux riches*, the silences and the difficulties of Chilean society. Donoso formed part of a generation of Chilean artists who reached maturity in the 1950s and 1960s and made a considerable impact outside their own country. Others of this period include the Surrealist painter Roberto Matta, whose strange, threatening figures took on a whole new depth of meaning after the events of 1973, or the internationally acclaimed pianist Claudio Arrau.

Cinema and Media

This kind of cosmopolitan confidence has largely disappeared from Chilean culture, which now often seems engaged in a narrow kind of provincialism, which is perhaps simply another expression of the effects of the turmoil of the past 30 years. Some areas of expression have almost completely ceased to exist, such as any kind of national cinema. Film-making was an integral part of the cultural upheaval of the Allende years, when the New Latin American Cinema was powerful throughout the continent. In Chile, films such as *The Jackal of Nahueltoro,* made by Miguel Littín, showed that there was the talent and the public to support Chilean films. The Popular Unity government set up a national film institute along the lines of the one in Cuba, but it was one of the prime targets for the military's repression, and after its destruction Chilean-made films disappeared almost entirely. Nowadays, Chile is like many other countries, where the national audience is not large enough to finance locally made films, and distributors are far more interested in showing the latest Hollywood productions as quickly as possible. It was only in 1997 that film censorship, imposed during the military regime, was finally lifted from the cinema.

A reverse process seems to have happened in the Chilean press. During the years of military rule, a number of opposition magazines flourished. Although they were often closed down, or their editors and journalists arrested, they kept alive political and social debate, and were eagerly awaited each week. Since the return of civilian rule, however, these magazines have mostly disappeared because they could no longer command a significant readership. As elsewhere, it seems to be the spread of television and videos which has adversely affected the written press, and Chilean television is as crass as that of most Latin American countries, with a huge proportion of soap operas, game shows, soccer, and with even news programs shortened or modified according to ratings.

Soccer

Soccer is the great sporting passion of the Chileans. Relatively few people go skiing or play tennis, but almost all males play or follow soccer, from mining communities at 10,000 feet up in the Andes to Tierra del Fuego. Teams with names like Everton or Santiago Wanderers show a clear British influence dating back to the early twentieth century, but the two main clubs are from the Catholic and the national universities, although they are professional rather than student teams. Passion for the game reached its height in 1962, when the soccer World Cup was held in Chile, and the national team succeeded for the first and only time in reaching the semi-finals (only to be beaten by the Brazilians). A more disappointing moment for Chilean soccer came in 1974, when the Soviet Union team refused to come to Chile because of the events of the previous year, and the national team won a walkover victory. In the 1990s, the craze for the sport is if anything even more pronounced, with some disapproving observers in Chile seeing this as yet another symptom of alienation from what they take to be the real values of Chilean society.

Food

But other values can still be found in another kind of cultural expression: Chilean food. Like much of the best cuisine, Chilean dishes are all the more delicious because cooks have had to use their art on humble basics: potatoes, corn, small pieces of meat, seafood. This has given rise to the meat pasty or *empanada;* to *cazuelas* or meat stews; to *humitas,* grains of corn cooked in their own husks; or the vast range of seafood combinations, of which perhaps the most justly famous is *curanto*, a thick stew with pork and whatever seafood is available, traditionally cooked in *nalca* leaves which look like giant rhubarb.

To return to poetry, Neruda's legendary appetite stretched to many of these other Chilean creations, as in his celebratory *Ode to Conger Eel Chowder:*

All that's needed now
is to add to this nectar

a few drops of cream
like a dense rose
then slowly
cook this treasure
until in the broth
all the essences of Chile
are warmed together,
then brought to table
the newly wedded
flavors
of sea and earth
so that in one dish
you may taste heaven.

WHERE TO GO, WHAT TO SEE

Most journeys to Chile begin in the capital Santiago, where the international airport is finally being updated and expanded. Santiago is a bustling, often congested, modern city, with few parts of great beauty or interest. The best views of it are from the top of the two hills which punctuate the urban landscape: the Cerro Santa Lucía close to the historical center, and the larger Cerro San Cristóbal. The Cerro Santa Lucía is a tastefully laid-out park with pleasant gardens and steeply climbing paths, good to test out the legs and the pollution levels in the air. At the top are mock battlements which offer a good vantage point for taking stock of the city center. The Cerro San Cristóbal is better for an afternoon stroll or a weekend picnic: it has a zoo on the lower slopes, and an excellent restaurant near the summit. Bellavista, the neighborhood close to the foot of the Cerro, is where many of the jazz and folk cafes of the capital are to be found, as well as the stores selling jewelry and handicrafts made from lapis lazuli, the typical Chilean semi-precious stone.

Elsewhere, much of the historical center has been pedestrianized. As in several other countries in Latin America, the relative absence of tourists in Chile means that it is possible to sit in one of the many cafes and watch the locals simply getting on with their business. There are few coach parties, organized tours, or heritage industry eyesores. The parks near the unfortunately canalized River Mapocho are well designed, with fine indigenous trees, and the National Fine Arts Museum set in the Parque Forestal has a considerable collection of paintings, as well as holding regular new exhibitions.

One of the most visited houses in Santiago is La Chascona, where the poet Pablo Neruda lived. This, like his house in Valparaíso or the rambling complex on the shores of the Pacific at Isla Negra, is stuffed with his collections (Neruda hoarded everything from ships' prows and shells to ornate glasses and risqué picture postcards) and gives a fascinating glimpse into the world of this century's most renowned Chilean. The cultures of previous centuries are on display at the Pre-Columbian Museum or at the Casa Colorada, which shows the history of the city.

The trip to Neruda's other home at Isla Negra is just one of the day outings from the capital which are well worth investigating. Isla Negra is not an island, but a rocky promontory jutting out into the Pacific. On it, Neruda built not just one house, but a whole warren of rooms, many with large glass windows facing out to the crashing sea. It was here that he died, a few days after the 1973 coup, doctors say of cancer, romantics say of a broken heart. The house was closed for many years under military rule, during which time many people scrawled messages of love or defiance on the rocks of the beach below, but it is now restored as a museum, with frequent poetry events. The best idea is to combine a visit to Isla Negra with lunch at a local restaurant, where the fresh seafood and a bottle or two of sparkling Chilean white wine are more or less guaranteed to bring out the poet in anyone.

Other excursions from the capital include a visit to one of the vineyards in the Central Valley, such as the Cousiño Macúl estate; some of the more traditional *fundos* or ranches are now taking guests, for riding or simply relaxation in the countryside. Another favorite of people from the capital is the Maipo Canyon, only about three-quarters of an hour away by car. There are small resorts dotted along the valley, where locally produced fruit, almonds, walnuts, and wine are sold at the roadside; at the far end of the canyon are hot springs at Baños Morales and Termas de Colina.

The other great attraction close to Santiago is of course the Andes mountains. They offer hiking, or more serious climbing; most Chileans, however, go for the skiing, which lasts from June through to October. It takes only an hour by car from Santiago to be right up in the mountains, where most of the smart modern resorts can be found. Among them are Farellones-El Colorado and Valle Nevado, the site of the 1993 Pan-American winter games. Portillo, beside the hopefully named Lagoon of the Inca, is one of most famous resorts throughout Latin America, and it was here that the world's fastest downhill ski run of 106 miles per hour was recorded. These are some of most cosmopolitan parts of Chile, with not only Brazilians and Argentines coming for ski holidays, but people from Australia, New Zealand, and the United States. Prices reflect the prosperity of the clientele.

In the summer, most people head out of Santiago the other way, down to the coast. Although it has a generally run-down feeling to it, the port of Valparaíso has much of the charm and some picturesque qualities lacking in the capital. In part, this is because much of the city clings to the steep hills, looking out over the vast Pacific Ocean. It is also because of the brightly-painted wooden houses and the narrow streets of the port, which give an immediate sense of history. Here too Neruda had a house, La Sebastiana, which in fact is more like a crow's nest, peering out to sea from the top of one of the city's many hills. The city is excellent to walk around, or you can take a cable car up from the harbor or a trip in a car or taxi round the Camino de Cintura, an avenue which meanders round near the top of the hillsides, as a perfect way to get an idea of the whole city. As an antidote, go and look at the new Congress building that President

Valdivia

Pinochet had built to keep the politicians out of the capital. Prepare to be horrified.

Most of Chile's Pacific resorts stretch up the coast north from Valparaíso. Almost adjacent to the city is the most traditional and stylish of them, Viña del Mar. From December to March, this chic place is full of Chileans anxious to show off their new-found prosperity in the casinos, at the racetrack, or at the famous annual song festival. Other resorts each have their own special character and devotees: boat owners, artists, politicians. The amount of development here in recent years has been quite phenomenal: many Chileans mutter under their breath about "drugs money" being laundered, but nothing has so far been proved. It should also be said that though the weather is often fine, and the seafood is always delicious, the Pacific Ocean is not especially warm, and can be quite dangerous for swimmers.

Beyond the Central Valley and coast, Chile presents very varied landscapes. To the north, the Andes and the Atacama desert offer an arid kind of beauty, where the freshness of the air and the stark mountain views are endlessly invigorating. It is also interesting to visit one of the enormous open-cast copper mines like Chuquicamata, which organizes tourist trips with free oxygen included in case the altitude is too much for you. It is also worth visiting one of the ghost towns such as the port of Pisagua, a booming place during the days of nitrate exports, now inhabited by only 200 people.

Otherwise, you can drive south down the Pan-American highway, or even take one of the few remaining trains which run down from Santiago, and head for the lake region. Here, because of the heavy rainfall, the Andes are wooded with native pine and of course the famous *araucaria* or "monkey puzzle" trees. Many of the lakes are part of a well-developed national parks system, where simple hotels, hostels, or camping are the norm. Some of the small lake towns here were settled by German or Swiss immigrants, and are surprisingly European in character, with tea shops, preserves, and German food. The volcano Mount Osorno dominates the scenery south of Puerto Montt, and close by, the Lakes Todos los Santos and Laguna Verde provide the opportunity to cross by boat into Argentina. Alternatively, a short ferry ride from Puerto Montt can take you across to the island of Chiloé, like a distant cousin of that other green land, Ireland, in the northern hemisphere.

Further south still, the rugged mountain landscapes have only recently become more accessible thanks to another legacy from the Pinochet era, the Carretera Austral or southern highway. Here there are still more spectacular volcanoes, lakes with glaciers in them, hot springs in the middle of nowhere. But the most popular destination is the Torres del Paine national park, where the *torres* or needles of rock thrust up from a landscape of snow and ice which is truly spectacular. The really determined can push on to the town of Punta Arenas, on the very southernmost tip of the mainland, or even explore the archipelago of Tierra del Fuego across the Straits of Magellan.

Those trips do require considerable organizing, as do visits to the two groups of islands out in the Pacific Ocean which are also part of Chile. The Juan Fernández islands, where the real-life Robinson Crusoe spent his lonely years far from civilization, are still remote, but can be reached by regular small airplane taxis or by boat. Even further out at more than 2,500 miles from Chile is Easter Island or Rapa Nui. It is now a five-hour trip from Santiago to the island, but in the great crater, with the giant, enigmatic statues staring up into the sky, the clutter, pollution, and noise of the Chilean capital seem several worlds away.

TIPS FOR TRAVELERS

Customs

In Chile, as in most Latin American countries, introductions are more formal than in Britain or the U.S. Women are greeted with a kiss on the cheek, men shake hands. This is repeated when people say goodbye. Chileans can be punctual for business appointments, but on social occasions they tend to think in terms of *hora latinoamericana*: it is seen as almost rude to arrive on time, as this suggests that your host cannot do without you, and that you have nothing better to do.

Safety

Chile is relatively safe compared to other Latin American countries. However, the centers of big cities such as Santiago or Valparaíso can be dangerous at night. On the beaches, it is unsafe to leave any belongings unattended. Unlike in some Latin American countries, the police and border guards very rarely accept bribes; they can also be extremely officious at airports and frontier controls.

Health

It is usually advisable to drink bottled water: although most Chileans drink tap water without problems, it can affect unsuspecting visitors badly. Care should also be taken with salads and vegetables, and soft fruit such as strawberries or grapes, as these are often irrigated and fertilized with untreated sewage when growing. Do not eat seafood directly from the beaches, as it is sometimes contaminated with what is called a *marea roja* (or "red tide"), which can make it poisonous.

Eating

Some of the best places to eat in Chile are in the markets, where the food is freshest. In more formal restaurants, the waiters expect a tip. Until recently, real coffee was something of a rarity in Chilean restaurants; do not be surprised if you are ceremoniously presented with a tin of instant coffee and a spoon if you order it. In Santiago, some of the best food is served in semi-clandestine restaurants known as *picadas*, to which you need to be invited by someone in the know.

Money

There is no problem changing foreign currency in Chile, but beware touts insisting on taking you to their own agency. Travelers' cheques often get a much lower rate than notes.

Shopping

There are many attractive shopping malls (*caracoles* or *moles*) in Santiago, stocked with all the well-known international labels. But more interesting are the markets and stores which specialize in handicrafts and local knitwear. The Bellavista district has a good selection, including El Almacén Campesiono, Purísima 303, which stocks pottery and finely wrought bronze and copper.

Taxis

Taxis in Santiago are cheap, although in the evenings a 50% surcharge is added. Drivers do not normally expect to be tipped.

Police

There are two branches of the police: the *carabineros*, who are in uniform and are in charge of traffic, public order etc. (known to most Chileans as the *pacos*), and the criminal police, who are in civilian clothing. Despite the years of military rule and curfew, both branches of the police are usually polite to foreign visitors.

ADDRESSES AND CONTACTS

Embassy of Chile,
1732 Massachusetts Avenue NW,
Washington DC 20036
Tel: (202) 785-1746

Embassy of Chile,
12 Devonshire Street,
London W1N 1FS
Tel: (0171) 580-6392
(tourist information available)

Journey Latin America,
14-16 Devonshire Road,
London W4 2BR
Tel: (0181) 747-3108

Instituto Chileno Norteamericano de Cultura,
Moneda 1467,
Santiago
Tel: 696-3215
(language courses, library, films)

FURTHER READING AND BOOKSTORES

Collins, J. and Lear, J., *Chile's Free-Market Miracle: A Second Look.* Oakland CA, 1995.

Constable P. and Valenzuela, A., *A Nation of Enemies: Chile Under Pinochet.* New York, 1991.

Drake, P.W. and Jaksic, I., *The Struggle for Democracy in Chile, 1982-1990.* Lincoln, NA, 1991.

Green, D., *Silent Revolution: The Rise of Market Economics in Latin America.* London, 1995.

Hojman, D., *Chile: The Political Economy of Development and Democracy in the 1990s.* Pittsburgh, 1993.

Loveman, B., *Chile: The Legacy of Hispanic Capitalism.* New York, 1979.

Meiselas, S. (ed), *Chile from Within.* New York, 1990.

O'Brien, P. and Roddick, J., *Chile: The Pinochet Decade.* London, 1983.

Timerman, J., *Chile: Death in the South.* New York, 1987.

Zammit, J.A., *The Chilean Road to Socialism.* Brighton, 1973.

Fiction and Poetry

Allende, I., *The House of the Spirits.* London and New York, 1985.

Donoso, J., *Curfew.* London and New York, 1990.

Neruda, P., *Canto General.* Berkeley, CA, 1991.

Poets of Chile: A Bilingual Anthology 1965-1985. Greensboro, NC, 1986.

Skármeta, A., *Burning Patience.* New York, 1987.

Local Bookstores

Librería Albers,
Merced 820,
Santiago

Librería Altamira,
Huérfanos 669,
Santiago

Librería Inglesa (Librería Kuatro),
Pedro de Valdivia 47,
Santiago

Librería Universitaria,
Esmeralda 1132,
Valparaíso

FACTS AND FIGURES

GEOGRAPHY

Official name: República de Chile.

Situation: Between the Andes mountain range and the Pacific seaboard of the south-west of Latin America. Bordered on to the north by Peru, to the east by Bolivia and Argentina.

Surface area: 292,135 square miles.

Administrative division: 12 regions (from north to south), plus the Metropolitan Region of Santiago. The regions are subdivided into 51 provinces.

Capital: Santiago de Chile: population 5,076,000 (including Gran Santiago conurbation), 1995.

Other principal cities (population x 1000, 1995 estimate): Concepción 350; Viña del Mar 322; Puente Alto 319; Valparaíso 282; Talcahuano 261; Temuco 239; Antofagasta 237; San Bernardo 206.

Infrastructure: In 1993, total length of roads was 49,430 miles, of which only 10% were classified as highways. The Pan American highway is the main north-south route, stretching 2,145 m.. An intensive road building programme has been undertaken to upgrade existing roads, and to add a further 600 m. of paved roads. In the mid-1990s, there were almost 4,400 m. of railroads in Chile, but no passenger services north of Santiago, except for a line to Bolivia. There is also an international line to Argentina (Antofagasta-Salta). Chile has two main international airports, Arturo Merino Benítez, close to the capital, and Arica airport. It also has 325 airfields. LAN-Chile and LADECO are the main aircarriers, both of them now privatized. Because of the country's extended coastline, maritime transport is extremely important, accounting for almost all foreign trade. The main ports are Valparaíso, Talcahuano, Antofagasta, Arica, Iquique, Puerto Montt and Punta Arenas.

Relief, landscape and climate: The fourth smallest territory in South America (after Ecuador, Paraguay, Uruguay, and the Guianas), Chile's varied geography is dominated by three features. Down the entire eastern border runs the Andean mountain chain, rising to over 19,000 feet. West of this is the Central Valley, which starts north of Santiago and continues for over 600 m. south of the capital to Puerto Montt. The third main feature is the coastline, with cliffs in the north, and heavily indented, flooded valleys in the south. In some areas, the coastline is separated from the central depression by a range of mountains. In the south there are many lakes and, as the climate grows colder, glaciers. The climate varies enormously according to longitude. In the northern desert, reaching down from the Peruvian border to the town of Copiapó, there is almost no rainfall. The country's nitrate deposits are concentrated here, together with copper mines, and only a few oases provide relief from the arid climatic conditions. The central regions have a temperate climate, with heavy rainfall in the winter months from May to September. This rainfall increases the further south one travels, and the weather becomes increasingly stormy and cold.

Flora and fauna: The animals and plant life of Chile are determined by the widely varying climate. In the desert north, vegetation is often sparse, comprised of cactuses, scrub and other unproductive woods. The lakes are often breeding grounds for flamingos and other aquatic birds, while in the mountains there are still fairly large numbers of guanacos, vicuñas and llamas. Members of the cat family such as pumas are now far rarer than 50 years ago, as is the archetypal bird of the Andes, the condor. In the south of Chile, there are still vast tracts of primary forest, some with continuous growth of several thousand years. There are many native species, such as the *araucaria* (monkey puzzle tree) and the *alerce* (Chilean larch). The heavy rainfall in these wooded regions helps create the conditions for a temperate rainforest, supporting a wide variety of plant life such as ferns, mosses, lianas, and a large number of small mammals, birds, and insects. The Chilean coastline is also the habitat for an abundant plant and animal life. There is a huge array of crustaceans, and a large seal and sea lion population. There used to be significant numbers of whales off the southern coast, but these have now been hunted almost to extinction.

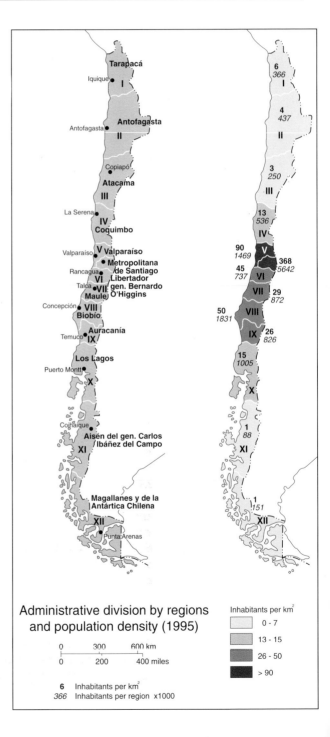

Administrative division by regions and population density (1995)

| 0 | 300 | 600 km |

| 0 | 200 | 400 miles |

6 Inhabitants per km^2
366 Inhabitants per region x1000

Inhabitants per km^2

- 0 - 7
- 13 - 15
- 26 - 50
- > 90

POPULATION

Population: 14.24 million (1992 census); 1996 estimate 14.46 million.
Annual population growth: 1.2% (1996); 1.8% (1960-1993).
Urbanization (1997): 84%.
Fertility (1996): a Chilean woman has an average of 2.2 children.
Age structure (1996): 0-14: 29%; 15-64: 65%; 65+ 6%.
Birthrate (1996): 18.09 per 1,000.
Mortality rate (1996): 5.68 per 1,000.
Infant mortality (1996): 15.6 per 1,000 live births.
Average life expectancy (1996): 74.5 years, men 71.25 years

and women 77.75 years.
Population per health professional (1997): 833.
Population with access to health services: 97%.
Education: primary education (8 years, starting at the age of 6) is free and compulsory. Secondary education is divided into the humanities-science program (4 years), geared towards university entrance, and the technical-professional program (6 years), leading to specialist training. Enrolment rates range from 100% at primary level and 75% at secondary to 19% at tertiary level. Current government spending on education is equivalent to approximately

3.6% of GDP. There are an increasing number of private universities, mostly offering vocational courses.
Illiteracy: 4.8% (1995 estimate)
Social development index: (UNDP Human Development Index 1996): Chile ranked 30th out of 175 countries, higher than Portugal or Costa Rica.
Ethnic composition: European and mestizo 92%; indigenous people 6%; others 2%.
Religion: 78% Roman Catholic; 10% estimated Evangelicals; 10 other Christian denominations.
Languages: Spanish, Aymara, Quechua, Mapuche and several other indigenous languages.

HISTORY AND POLITICS

Key historical dates: c. 1450: Incas move from Peru into Chile; unable to conquer indigenous Mapuche in south of country * 1520: Ferdinand Magellan's voyage of discovery * 1541: city of Santiago founded by Pedro de Valdivia* 1553: death of Valdivia at hands of Mapuche * 1598: Mapuche begin war against Spanish colonizers * 1817-1818: Bernardo O'Higgins leads independence forces against Spanish, victories at Chacabuco and Maipú * 1818: independence of Chile declared * 1833: creation of civilian constitution * 1843:

Chile lays claim to Magellan straits * 1879-1883: War of the Pacific; Chile gains valuable nitrate regions from Bolivia and Peru * 1880: final pacification of the Mapuche * 1886-1891: modernizing presidency of José Manuel Balmaceda * 1907: massacre of trade unionists at Iquique * 1920-1924: first presidency of Arturo Alessandri * 1924-1932: military coup and army-backed regime of Carlos Ibáñez * 1932-1938: Alessandri's second term * 1938: Popular Front government elected * 1940s: copper becomes Chile's main export

* 1949: female franchise introduced * 1957: founding of Christian Democrat Party * 1964-1970: reforming government of Christian Democrat Eduardo Frei * 1970: election of Salvador Allende * 11.9.1973: military coup against Allende's Popular Unity government; death of Allende * 1977-: start of "economic miracle" * 1980: General Pinochet's constitution approved by plebiscite * 1981: severe recession * 1986: failed assassination attempt on Pinochet * 1988: plebiscite votes against Pinochet's continuation in power *

1989: election of Christian Democrat Patricio Aylwin *
1993: Eduardo Frei wins election.
Constitution: presidential republic. President is elected by popular vote every six years. Bicameral Congress, with a lower chamber of 120 deputies elected every four years, and a Senate of both elected and appointed senators, who serve an eight-year term. Former presidents are senators for life.
Head of State: Eduardo Frei Ruiz-Tagle (to end 1999).
Main political groupings (with seats in Chamber of Deputies and Senate after December 1993 elections): Partido Demócrata Cristiano (PDC) 37 (13); Renovación Nacional (RN) 29 (11); Partido Socialista de Chile 15 (5); Unión Demócrata Independiente (UDI) 15 (3); Partido por la Democracia 15 (2); others 8 (4).
Armed forces (1995): total 99,000 (army 54,000; navy 25,000; air force 11,000); expenditure: $1,900 million, 3.8% of GDP (7.8% in 1985).
Membership of international organizations: United Nations and UN organizations; Organization of American States (OAS); SELA (Latin American Integration System); IDB (Inter-American Development Bank); associate member of Mercosur.
Media and communications: More than 120 newspapers appearing twice a week or more. *El Mercurio* and *Las Ultimas Noticias*, both based in Santiago, have the largest circulations. Five television stations, all of them now privately owned. In 1992, around 3 million households had television. There are an estimated 450 radio stations, with 345 sets per 1,000 population.
Telephone ownership: 11 per 100.

ECONOMY

Unit of currency: peso (exchange rate perUS$1: 420 (1997); 407 (1995); 362 (1992); 349 (1991).
Gross Domestic Product (GDP): $65 billion (1995)
GDP per capita: $ 3,576 (1996)
GDP growth: 6.3% (1993); 3.2% (1994); 8.5% (1995); 7% (1996); 5.8% (1997).
GDP per sector (1990): services 56.2%; industry 36.4%; agriculture 7.4%.
Inflation: 1993: 12.2%; 1994: 12%; 1995: 7.9%; 1996: 6.5%.
Unemployment (1995): 5.4%.
Exports (1996): $15.35 billion; principal exports: copper, other metals and minerals; wood products; fish and fishmeal; fruits.
Imports (1996): $16.50 billion (1995); principal imports: capital goods; machinery and spare parts; raw materials; petroleum and petroleum products; foodstuffs.
Trade balance (1996): -$1.15 billion.
Current account balance (1996): -$2.52 billion.
Principal trading partners (1995): exports European Union (UK, Germany, France, Spain, etc.) 26.5%, Latin America (Argentina, Brazil, Peru) 18.7%, Japan 17.7%, U.S. 14.6%; imports U.S. 19%, Japan 8%, Brazil 8%, Germany 7%, others 58%.
Foreign debt: $20.8 billion (1996 estimate).